AWAKENING THE
SLUMBERING
SPIRIT

AWAKENING THE SLUMBERING SPIRIT

JOHN LOREN & PAULA
SANDFORD
AND LEE BOWMAN

Charisma
HOUSE
A STRANG COMPANY

Most Strang Communications/Charisma House/Christian House/Christian Life/Excel Books/FrontLine/Realms/Siloam products are available at special quantity discounts for bulk purchase for sales promotions, premiums, fund-raising, and educational needs. For details, write Strang Communications/Charisma House/Christian Life/Excel Books/FrontLine/Realms/Siloam, 600 Rinehart Road, Lake Mary, Florida 32746, or telephone (407) 333-0600.

Awakening the Slumbering Spirit
    by John Loren and Paula Sandford and Lee Bowman
Published by Charisma House
A Strang Company
600 Rinehart Road
Lake Mary, Florida 32746
www.strangdirect.com

Unless otherwise noted, all Scripture quotations are from the Holy Bible, New International Version. Copyright © 1973, 1978, 1984, International Bible Society. Used by permission.

Scripture quotations marked KJV are from the King James Version of the Bible.

Scripture quotations marked NAS are from the New American Standard Bible. Copyright © 1960, 1962, 1963, 1968, 1971, 1972, 1973, 1975, 1977 by the Lockman Foundation. Used by permission. (www.Lockman.org)

Design Director: Bill Johnson
Cover Designer: Justin Evans

Library of Congress Cataloging-in-Publication Data

Sandford, John Loren.
 Awakening the slumbering spirit / John Loren and Paula Sandford and
Lee Bowman.
    p. cm.
 Rev. ed. of: Waking the slumbering spirit.
 Includes bibliographical references (p.   ).
 ISBN 978-1-59979-341-2
 1. Spiritual life--Christianity. 2. Religious awakening--Christianity. I.
Sandford, Paula. II. Bowman, Lee. III. Sandford, John Loren. Waking
the slumbering spirit. IV. Title.

 BV4509.5.S263 2008
 243--dc22

                        2008021201

08 09 10 11 12 — 987654321
Printed in the United States of America

CONTENTS

Part I

Understanding the Personal Spirit

1

SLEEPWALKING IN THE SPIRIT

TEN-YEAR-OLD MATTHEW GREW INCREASINGLY concerned about the slender tabby that had been showing up each evening at the kitchen door. The cat would sit nervously on the porch step, staring into the house in hope that Matthew would feed his other cats outside and that there would be food left in their bowls. Waiting impatiently in the cold night air, she would stare at him through the storm door with big green eyes reflecting the warm light from within the house. If he approached to get a better look, she would retreat into the shadows. When he would take her a fresh bowl of food, she would run away and hide until the glass door once again separated them and she could safely come to eat.

Matthew named his timid visitor Fraidie, short for "Fraidie-cat." He tried his best to coax her into friendliness with sweet talk and food offered in his outstretched hand. But Fraidie was wild and would not respond. Born somewhere under a house or in a neighborhood shed, she had never experienced the taming effect of human touch. She grew up wary and afraid, living a tenuous life of scavenging at his back door and making a bad-weather home in his family's garage by climbing through one of the garage door windows Matthew had kicked out with his soccer ball.

Some months later the inevitable happened, and Fraidie became a mother in the garage. Matthew had suspected as much but nevertheless was surprised one Saturday morning to see a fat waddling ball of fur scurrying behind some boxes and old bicycles in the dark garage. A thorough search produced one kitten that had not survived and a cute, very frightened little female that he decided had to be rescued from the kind of life her mother was leading.

 Our world is sadly lacking the kind of loving nurture that produces fully functional adults with alive and responsive personal spirits.

Matthew brought the nearly weaned kitten inside, and with the help of his family, she made the transition to solid food after a few days of eyedropper milk feedings. The weeks that followed were filled with real wonder. The scared and trembling kitten quickly warmed to being held and touched. By day she would frolic and play for hours with Matthew on the floor. By night she would snuggle up against the family's seventeen-year-old blind and deaf poodle, getting warmth and comfort from a surrogate canine mom.

No longer an untouchable fraidie-cat doomed to a life of lonely scavenging, the kitten quickly took her place as a full member of the family. She became wonderfully alive in her spirit, playfully affectionate, and flourishing in every way as she grew. In touching tribute to her mother, Matthew named the kitten Lady—a name to rhyme with Fraidie, but so distinctly different.

What does this story have to do with the slumbering spirit? It is a kind of parable that you must open your spiritual ears to hear. God has so much to reveal to those who will listen and for those who can open their hearts to His continuing words of instruction on how to become more fully human.

Fraidie's kitten became "Lady the family member" because she came into the proper kind of loving nurture that transformed her from a wild creature into a loving pet. That message, translated into human development, is a prophetic message from God. Our world is sadly lacking in similar loving nurture that could produce fully functional adults with alive and responsive personal spirits. Knowing what to do about this problem begins with recognizing that the problem exists.

Sounding the alarm about this is as much a prophetic task as that of the Old Testament prophets in calling Israel back into proper relationship with God.

KEYS OF KNOWLEDGE

The role of a prophet is to deliver the word of God to His people. A prophet admonishes, warns, directs, intercedes, teaches, and counsels. He stands at the walls to see what the Lord is doing so that he might call the body of Christ to respond appropriately.

Some may suggest that as a result of the mission and ministry of Jesus, God did away with prophets and prophecy because they were no longer needed. This is not so. Instead, God has expanded the prophet's function and power by virtue of what Jesus accomplished on the cross and through His resurrection. A prophet should no longer be conceived of as the lonely watchman on the wall of his culture.

God has redirected the role of the prophet so that he can now be an integral part of the church, whose role is to carry on the work of Christ in bringing the world into rightful relationship with God. The church, through the guidance of the Holy Spirit, should cherish the prophetic role and protect its prophets, giving them support structures to more effectively reach the people in need of God's Word.

One of the important functions of the prophetic role is to listen carefully to God so as to receive "keys of knowledge" that God has for His people. The prophet then interprets God's word so that men and women might see more clearly how to come into closer relationship and greater freedom with their Lord. Luke 11:52 explains this more clearly: "Woe to you experts in the law, because you have taken away the key to knowledge. You yourselves have not entered, and you have hindered those who were entering."

> *While God's laws are always to be obeyed, repressive human additions to morals and misapplied guilt are often major factors in sabotaging the freedom that should come with the experience of rebirth in Jesus Christ.*

Life is complex. Even though we strive to seek God's leadership, it is not easy to make our way in this world with a sense of God-directed purpose. When value systems get confused and when sin and circumstances entrap us, we need the clarity of God's vision to find our way and to be set free to live as He would like us to live. Prophets provide the keys of knowledge for that clarity of vision.

Unfortunately, empty religiosity and legalistic adherence to laws and rituals have always served as obstacles to the spiritual freedom God wants us to achieve. In the time of Christ, the Pharisees were very zealous in their attempts to promote righteousness among the people. But Jesus condemned them because even when they were not hypocritical, they tended to "load people down with burdens they can hardly carry" (Luke 11:46).

God does not want to load us down with hopeless burdens of behavioral rules. While God's laws are always to be obeyed, repressive human additions to morals and misapplied guilt are often major factors in sabotaging the freedom that should come with the experience of rebirth in Jesus Christ. What we all need are keys of knowledge that will help us to understand where we are and why we are in the condition we are in. We need to meet our Lord in a very personal way and unlock our deepest beings to live in the spirit and the truth of God. We need to be awakened to the wonder of Jesus Christ living in us and bringing us into the fullness of our humanity.

Most people in the world today are lost in a sea of ambiguity. Our contemporary culture deafens us with the noise of conflicting values and ideologies. People have no sense of certainty on which to anchor their lives and establish priorities. The Lord sent us into this ministry a long time ago as prophets, working at first in the pastorate, then founding Elijah House Ministries for prayer ministry, and subsequently teaching and writing with a ministry that has stretched around the world. During our many years of prayer ministry, thousands of people have come to us to seek ways to put their shattered lives back together. During these years of listening to both the hurts of men and women and to the voice of God, we have been given a number of keys of knowledge to interpret to the church.

Performance orientation

Performance orientation, one of the most common maladies throughout the world, consists of a pervasive need to please others and perform up to the expectations of others. This means striving to perform for wrong motives—to win love and a sense of belonging when those have already been given.

The result is a compulsive work ethic, preoccupation with doing everything right, an inordinate desire to be liked or approved of, and dissatisfaction with yourself for what you have achieved as opposed to who you are as a person. In Christians, it is rooted in an inability to believe God can love us unless we work for it. Those who were not nurtured as children can be especially tempted toward performing for love.

Bitter-root judgment and expectancy

A surprising consequence can develop by making judgments and harboring ill will toward parents or others with whom you have significant relationships. Judgments can turn inward as bitter roots and produce the same behavioral tendencies in yourself that you found hurtful and destructive from others!

For instance, when you were a child, if your parents rarely hugged you or said, "I love you," you probably felt resentful. If you did not forgive, and a bitter-root judgment formed in your heart, you may now be doing to your children what your parents did to you—failing to hug or tell them you love them. For in shutting your heart toward your parents, you shut your heart toward God, preventing it from receiving the nurture He would give to make up for their lack. Psalm 27:10 says, "Though my father and mother forsake me, the LORD will receive me." Your heart became impenetrable and incapable of receiving what you needed. Now, as an adult, you cannot pass on to your children what you did not receive.

You unknowingly act out your own judgments. You may also have come to expect things to be a certain way, and consequently they always seem to turn out the way you expect them to. This causes you to reap by immutable law the results of what you have sown in judgments. For instance, if you judged your parents for ignoring you, you may reap that judgment by unconsciously expecting others to ignore you as well. Others may pick up on that message and respond accordingly. Uncannily, even people who are normally attentive toward others tend to overlook you or leave you out of their plans.

Inner vows

When you experience hurt in your childhood, a common reaction is to employ emotional self-defense by making an inner vow that you will never let yourself be vulnerable in that way again. This emotional barrier then can shut you off from fulfilling relationships because your inner self will never let go enough to trust and risk in vulnerability.

This may play out in a number of ways: to keep from feeling hurt about the hugs you missed, you may have vowed not to need hugs, reasoning that since you don't need them in the first place, you can't be hurt when you don't receive them. That put up an emotional barrier between you and others and dampened your spirit's ability to experience a hug. Now, as an adult, you may be incapable of feeling that special something that passes heart to heart and spirit to spirit through an embrace. Or maybe you vowed not to need the "I love yous" you rarely heard. Now as an adult, you may not be able to accept or feel the effects of an "I love you" when it is offered. Your spirit can fall asleep to the ability to feel and experience the blessings of life and love.

Heart of stone

Sinful reactions to years of neglect or hurt can cause emotional callousness to develop, protecting the inner person from further hurt by stifling real feelings, avoiding vulnerability, blocking out tenderness, and refusing to listen or be sensitive to the needs of others. This is often characterized by rugged individualism born of cynicism, resulting in emotional impenetrability.

Wounded burden bearing

Occasionally, even a person with a sensitive inborn temperament can end up slumbering spiritually. A naturally sensitive person tends to pick up and carry others' feelings without even trying. There is danger in burden bearing because if not properly handled, it can wound your spirit and drain you of life. But when burdens are properly carried through intercessory prayer and by being in touch with refreshment from the Lord, burden bearing is the key to fullness of life. In the most positive sense, burden bearers are those who consciously seek out the hurts of others in order to transmit those hurts to the Lord for healing.

But there are those who never learn to do this. Many do not even learn to distinguish others' feelings from their own. After encountering a friend who is hiding hurt behind a smile, such a person can absorb that hurt and come away thinking it is his own. He can think to himself, "My friend didn't look hurt, so these feelings must be coming from me." Baffled at why he accountably feels this way, he is unable to process and release the pain. If a child grows up this way with no one to help him identify and release burdens, he may choose to shut down the pain he feels, and with it, the ability to feel and experience life and love.

The slumbering spirit

A slumbering spirit results in the crippling of one's ability to function in many areas of daily living. Among the consequences of slumbering in the spirit are a lack of a true conscience, inability to communicate intimately and to sustain close relationships, inability to worship and have a fulfilling devotional life, inability to learn from the past or project into the future, and inability to sustain good health.

Persons slumbering in spirit are usually unaware there is so much more depth to life than they are experiencing.

Slumbering in spirit can be caused in two ways. Closing the heart in reaction to poor nurture in childhood causes the personal spirit to be stunted just as a flower is stunted without proper nutrients. In adulthood, the personal spirit can fall asleep through neglect of prayer and devotional life, by withdrawing from intimacy with others, by falling into repeated sin, and/or by ceasing to participate in the wonders of recreational fun, nature, art, and music.

The purpose of this book is to explore the concept of the slumbering spirit, not just to understand what it is and what causes it, but also to suggest ways the human spirit can be awakened and nurtured into the vitality of the healthy living God intends.

Awakening the Slumbering Spirit portrays how a slumbering personal spirit can be detected and suggests many ways in which Christians can overcome this debilitating condition in their lives. A number of important terms will be defined in this first chapter. Later chapters will then describe why the spirit slumbers, illustrate characteristics of an awakened spirit, and suggest ways to keep a child's spirit awake or to reawaken the spirit of a slumbering adult. We have also designed spirit-awakening exercises at the end of each chapter. It is important that you work through these with a loving, mature Christian friend or prayer minister who can help grow the needed qualities in you. You may find that the small group you attend at your church is open to doing these exercises and that other members in your group need to be awakened as well. One thing we must recognize is that being awakened to life is not something you can only do alone. God made it so that through the interaction of one person with another we can draw each other out and into life through the unfailing love of Christ working itself through us.

Understanding the Slumbering Spirit

An understanding of the slumbering spirit is a powerful and incisive key of knowledge God has given us to help set people free. This concept was discovered the hard way by struggling unsuccessfully to help many people over the years through counseling and prayer ministry. A number of people seemingly could not experience a breakthrough of healing and growth in their lives.

Although we applied our most thoughtful prayer ministry techniques and all the intellectual and spiritual resources we knew of, it seemed they just could not break away from ingrained patterns of destructive attitudes and behavior. They sincerely came looking for help and were willing to try whatever we would suggest, but they could not function in some areas of life essential for personal growth and in sustaining healthy relationships with others.

We had been particularly puzzled because many of the people we ministered to seemed to be equipped better than most with the resources needed to succeed in life. One might describe them as Bible-believing, church-attending Christians who attempted to love and serve others. But in some areas of their being, it was as though cogs were missing. Their behavior proved to be erratic and unpredictable, and they would surprise everyone regularly with decisions and actions that contradicted their professed beliefs as Christians.

Many of these people seemed incapable of understanding cause-and-effect relationships. They couldn't make the connection that certain patterns of behavior produce predictably destructive consequences for themselves and others. Characteristically, they lived only for the moment and appeared incapable of avoiding the kind of decisions that would invariably get them into trouble and wound the lives and spirits of their loved ones.

A striking example of this was a young man who, along with his wife, came to us for prayer ministry. He seemed to have everything going for him. He clearly loved his wife and children. As a member of a charismatic church, he was Holy Spirit–filled, Bible-believing, and active in church activities. But he was always getting into trouble because he would not pay his bills. He would buy things on credit and then neglect to make payments when the bills came due. When creditors would call, he would become absolutely furious because he felt they had no right to bother him! He seemed to have no awareness or conscience about what not paying his bills did to other people.

Every once in a while he would also become sexually involved with other women with no apparent conscience about the morality of his behavior. He had no sense that his adulterous actions would wound the heart of the Lord or wound his wife and his relationship with his family. After many frustrating ministry sessions, he had us crying out to God: "What's the matter here? Why doesn't this guy take responsibility for paying his bills? Why doesn't he seem to have a conscience about his immoral behavior?"

During this same period, we were traveling a great deal, often crossing trails with some well-known evangelists and preachers who were holding services in churches across the country. In our conversations with church people in those local communities, we were surprised to learn that several of these religious celebrities had reputations as womanizers, becoming sexually involved with women in almost every community they visited. The result, of course, was a great deal of anguish and hurt among the church people in those communities, and disillusionment among the fragile new believers who had been moved to faith by these representatives of God.

 The fact that a man's ministry works miracles doesn't mean that his own life is righteous. Men do not cause miracles to happen—it is God who performs miracles.

We found ourselves again crying out to God: "How can this be? How can men like this, who really believe in and sacrificially serve the Lord, fail to possess a moral conscience about what they do? How can they allow their Christian witness to be so jeopardized by their immoral actions?"

Concerning this matter of men and women of God acting in ungodly ways, you need to understand that the gifts and the calling of God are irrevocable, or permanent (Rom. 11:29). That is to say, when God gives a gift or a calling, He doesn't take it back. When a person works a miracle through God's power, it says nothing about the character of the person. The miracle speaks of the character of God.

That is a very difficult concept for some people to understand because we often attribute more importance to the personality of the message bearer than to the content and power of the message itself. We are not saved or healed by a preacher; we are saved or healed by the power of God. The preacher is just the instrument through which the Holy Spirit works to reach us. God can work perfect miracles through rascals, and He often does.

The validity of one's baptism does not depend on the righteousness of the priest or pastor who performed the baptism. Your baptism is between you and God. The power of the sacrament is dependent solely on God's grace. Similarly, the oneness you experience with Jesus Christ through Communion is not dependent on whether the minister who serves you happens to be righteous. He may be a rascal, but the Communion is perfectly valid because God vindicates the position. God acts anyway.

The fact that a man's ministry works miracles doesn't mean that his own life is righteous. Men do not cause miracles to happen, and they should not be revered as though they have that power. It is God who performs miracles, and He sometimes chooses to do it through those who may seem unworthy by our earthly standards.

Confused, hurt, and disappointed about Christians who seemed to live with no conscience, we asked God for an answer in what by that time had become our fervent prayer: we simply cried, "HELP!" God heard our cry and answered.

The answer God revealed through prayer and Scripture study was this: *these persons are slumbering in their personal spirit.* The Lord further revealed that if someone has a slumbering spirit, he or she becomes incapable of functioning adequately in those areas of life in which the spirit affects people at the deepest level. Among these are the conscience, building and sustaining personal relationships, intimate communication, and devotional life. The mind still works. Emotions still work. But the spirit is dysfunctional because it is in a sleep state.

By looking more closely at the Scriptures, we saw many references to the slumbering spirit that we had never been aware of before.

> But everything exposed by the light becomes visible, for it is light that makes everything visible. This is why it is said: "Wake up, O sleeper, rise from the dead, and Christ will shine on you."
>
> —EPHESIANS 5:13–14

We had read this Bible passage many times before, with the perception that these fledgling Ephesian Christians were simply being admonished by Paul to get serious, try harder, and put their immorality behind them. But on closer look, we saw much more. These were slumbering spirits—Christian believers so entrapped in their lifestyle that Paul likened them to zombies who needed to be awakened from the dead so the light of Christ might shine on them.

Whether stunted in the spirit from reactions to a lack of loving nurture as children or falling into sleep as adults by fleeing from affection and neglecting worship and prayer, the effects are the same. The personal spirit becomes locked in a shadowy world of unawareness. The mind and emotions may be awake, but the person is sleepwalking in the spirit.

Escaping from this trap of darkness is not accomplished by the intellectual act of saying, "I believe," or even by working very hard at being a moral person. The spirit must be awakened and nurtured again through inner healing, committed discipleship, and the patient love of friends and family.

Awakening must begin with awareness of the slumbering state you find yourself in. The awakening grows as you learn new behaviors such as the ones Paul catalogs in the fifth chapter of Ephesians. As these new ways are learned, the spirit will awaken and the light of Jesus Christ will shine on and through you.

1. Be careful and choose wisely how you will live (v. 15).

2. Find out what pleases the Lord and be imitators of Christ (vv. 1, 10).

3. Stay away from intoxicants that drug your senses and make you susceptible to immorality (v. 18).

4. Seek opportunities for lightheartedness with laughter, singing, and Spirit-filled fun (v. 19).

5. Give thanks to God for everything life brings (v. 20).

6. Submit to each other in love and trust as Christian brothers and sisters (v. 21).

7. Be honorable in your family relationships, treating others with respect and consideration (vv. 22–23).

8. Seek the Lord for strength, nourishing, and cherishing. Be confident in His power to nurture and protect you (vv. 25, 29–32).

In the months following, God answered our prayer. Our search of the Scriptures continued to reveal the truth of this concept. The spirit slumbers in the lives of so many people. Many in Christ's church, even leaders, are like dreamers. In Isaiah 56:10 we found, "Israel's watchmen are blind, they all lack knowledge; they are all mute dogs, they cannot bark;

they lie around and dream, they love to sleep." And again, in Romans 13:11–14, the Scriptures say, "The hour has come for you to wake up from your slumber, because our salvation is nearer now than when we first believed. The night is nearly over; the day is almost here. So let us put aside the deeds of darkness and put on the armor of light. Let us behave decently, as in the daytime, not in orgies and drunkenness, not in sexual immorality and debauchery, not in dissension and jealousy. Rather, clothe yourselves with the Lord Jesus Christ, and do not think about how to gratify the desires of the sinful nature."

Please understand: if our spirits are awake, we put on Jesus and walk in Jesus's nature. If our spirits fall asleep, we put on the flesh and walk in the flesh.

> Awake, awake, O Zion,
>   clothe yourself with strength.
> Put on your garments of splendor,
>   O Jerusalem, the holy city.
> The uncircumcised and defiled
>   will not enter you again.
> Shake off your dust;
>   rise up, sit enthroned, O Jerusalem.
> Free yourself from the chains on your neck,
>   O captive Daughter of Zion.
>
> —ISAIAH 52:1–2

But you, brothers, are not in darkness so that this day should surprise you like a thief. You are all sons of the light and sons of the day. We do not belong to the night or to the darkness. So then, let us not be like others, who are asleep, but let us be alert and self-controlled.

—1 THESSALONIANS 5:4–6

Can you imagine the church with a grand case of insomnia trying to stay awake until the Lord comes? Paul isn't talking about physical sleep, is he? He is talking about spiritual slumber.

Behold, I come like a thief! Blessed is he who stays awake and keeps his clothes with him, so that he may not go naked and be shamefully exposed.

—REVELATION 16:15

When we fall asleep spiritually, we lose those garments of Jesus Christ and walk about in the shame of our flesh. With this newfound key of knowledge of the slumbering spirit fresh in our minds, we went out into the body of Christ to teach from our awareness. But to our chagrin, we found that most people had little or no understanding of the specific functions of the personal spirit contrasted to the functions of the soul, thoughts, and emotions of our minds and the inter-relatedness of our bodies to spirit, mind, and soul.

This was true of nearly everyone, including those in the church as well as those out in the secular world. To more fully understand what it means to have a slumbering spirit, let's begin with some basic definitions of those elements that make up our being.

Our personal spirit

The root meaning of both the Hebrew and Greek words for *spirit* (*ruach* and *pneuma*) is a movement of air or wind.

> The Spirit of God moved upon the face of the waters.
>
> —GENESIS 1:2, KJV

The spirit is the life principle or energy of all life. Our personal spirit is that which God has breathed into us from the beginning.

> The LORD God formed the man from the dust of the ground and breathed into his nostrils the breath of life, and the man became a living being.
>
> —GENESIS 2:7

Jesus said to Nicodemus:

> Flesh gives birth to flesh, but the Spirit gives birth to spirit. You should not be surprised at my saying, "You must be born again." The wind blows wherever it pleases. You hear its sound, but you cannot tell where it comes from or where it is going. So it is with everyone born of the Spirit.
>
> —JOHN 3:6–8

This passage reflects a play on words since the Greek word used can be translated both as *wind* and as *spirit*. Genesis 1:27 tells us that man is created in the image of God, meaning that man is like God by nature. We can take this to indicate that man is a moral being and has intelligence and free will.

From a Christian point of view, being in God's image indicates the possibility for mankind to be transformed into the personality of Christ.

> For those God foreknew he also predestined to be conformed to the likeness of his Son, that he might be the firstborn among many brothers.
>
> —ROMANS 8:29

> And we, who with unveiled faces all reflect the Lord's glory, are being transformed into his likeness with ever-increasing glory, which comes from the Lord, who is the Spirit.
>
> —2 CORINTHIANS 3:18

The image of man in Hebrew thought was much less complex than New Testament thinking, which provides a more expansive view of spirit and soul. Paul wrote to a people versed in Greek philosophy, and he attempted to combat their dualistic concept that the spirit and the body are separate—the spirit being good and the body evil. In Hebrew thinking there was no separation of the soul into body, heart (mind), and spirit. The soul was the personality, or even the entire person, and one reasoned from one's heart. Wisdom, insight, inspiration, and courage came from the presence of God's Spirit. This spiritual nature of man to the Hebrew people was perceived in terms of their covenant relationship with God, who would be present with them if they proved to be faithful to His will.

As Paul interpreted man and God to the more philosophical Greek culture of the first century, he portrayed what might be viewed as a triangle of personality in each person:

- Mind—that which comprises our will and our reason

- Flesh—a word sometimes referring to our body but used by Paul to mean selfish desire and bodily lusts. We commonly strive to restrain our "flesh" through the law.

- Spirit—the inner being; the precious life energy breathed into us by God

Paul taught that these functions of our being are inseparably linked and are likely to do battle with each other until our spirit is renewed and we are transformed into the likeness of Christ. Our selfish desires can only be overcome through the power of God's grace. Then the mind and flesh are brought into harmony with Christ's will.

Paul portrays the spirit of man as that through which the Holy Spirit of God can indwell a person. The Holy Spirit comforts, protects, inspires, and equips us with spiritual gifts to do God's reconciling work in the world. Our personal spirit is eternal. It will return to God, the Scripture says, and the body will return to the dust (Eccles. 12:7).

The most beautiful image imaginable is Jesus, through His Holy Spirit, standing at our spirit's door and knocking. Are we awake enough to hear, to rejoice, and to open the door thankfully and journey with Him? Or do we sleep unaware of the wonderful life He has prepared for us?

Our soul

In Genesis 2:7 Scripture speaks of God breathing the breath of life (the spirit) into man and man becoming a living being (or soul). In many ways the words *spirit* and *soul* are used interchangeably in scriptural translations to refer to the life principle or life energy. A Hebrew would not speak of himself as having a body. Rather, he would speak in terms of being a soul (an animated psychophysical being in a fleshly form).

To portray the inner being or the life energy within a person, the term *spirit* was most often used. Unusual energy, skill, or inspiration was usually attributed to the presence of the Spirit of God. On the other hand, the term *soul* was most often used to refer to desire, appetite, or emotional experiences. The soul hungers and thirsts. The soul is satisfied or feels joy, sorrow, hope, or despair.

As Christians, we can define the soul in general terms as that structure of the heart, mind, character, and personality that we build. We build the soul as our spirit encounters life, reacts, and develops coping mechanisms. The soul is the expression of our personality with which we make our way in the world. At times, it can be a temple through which our spirit finds beautiful expression. At other times, our soul can be a self-imposed prison of hatred, despair, resentment, or lust. And on still other occasions, our soul can be a battle tank in which we seek refuge while aggressively attacking outsiders who are considered to be a threat.

Our mind

The mind is our intellect, our decision-making capability, our reasoning and logical self that chooses a course of action. In ancient Hebrew thought, the seat of intellect was considered to be the heart. However, the thinking heart (intellect) was more practical than speculative. Thoughts moved to action. They were not for doing battle in the realm of conflicting logic, as would be the case in New Testament times and even more so today.

In New Testament terminology, the mind is identified as the heart's reasoning capacity, often in tension with one's feelings or flesh. The mind is subject to bad judgment and foolish decisions and yet capable of transformation into harmony with one's God-directed spirit.

Many New Age thinkers today elevate intellect to godlike status, referring to the "universal mind" as being the god force itself in which we all share a mystical and synergistic destiny. However, New Testament revelations in the writings of Paul speak of an all-powerful and personal God who is in full control of His creation and who has made provision for man to be brought into loving relationship with Him more than just mentally.

Our mind is a God-given gift of intelligence and free choice that we can opt to squander or to invest. It is an integral part of our being; in combination with our body, soul, and spirit, it can be brought into harmony with God's will.

Our body

At first thought, it may seem foolish to construct a definition of the human body since we seem to be so familiar with our own flesh and blood. But in familiarity, we may have allowed ourselves to become overly simplistic in our perception of what our bodies are. The scientific community is in virtual agreement that we have only now begun to scratch the surface of understanding the mysteries of how the human body operates. From a physical standpoint, our bodies are incredible machines. But our bodies are so much more than chemistry and physics. There is an interrelatedness of body and spirit that cannot be measured in laboratory experiments.

When we abuse our bodies through overwork, stress, fatigue, diet, drugs, and poor hygiene, we suffer more than physical consequences. Our body "on tilt" affects our entire system. We are unable to think clearly. Our judgment is impaired. We become emotionally volatile. Depression sets in. We go into spiritual turmoil.

We are, in fact, much as the ancient Hebrews assumed us to be—an inseparable unity of spirit, soul, mind, and body. To understand this unity is to more clearly understand what the Scripture says in referring to our bodies as holy temples.

The Personal Spirit and the Holy Spirit

Some have asked what the relationship is between the personal spirit and the Holy Spirit. Does being filled with the Holy Spirit automatically cause an awakening of the personal spirit?

This question can be answered in a more perceptive way by stepping back and defining several terms frequently used in Christian circles but misunderstood by many. These terms are *evangelicals, charismatics, Pentecostals, speaking in tongues, interpretation of tongues, spiritual gifts,* and *fruit of the Spirit.*

A discussion of each of these could certainly fill a book of its own, and you can find ample reference material to do a full study on each of these areas if you wish. These issues are addressed here to clarify how the Holy Spirit impacts the life of individual Christians, how the role of the Holy Spirit is interpreted in different church groups, and the relationship this has to an awakened personal spirit.

Evangelical refers to those Christian people who know, have experienced, and teach what it is to be born anew—to receive Jesus as Lord and Savior.

Charismatic describes those who know and have experienced that rebirth in Jesus Christ but also know what it is to have the Holy Spirit released within them. This means basically the exercising of spiritual gifts in one's life as tools of ministry.

The charismatic understanding of the Holy Spirit's presence has been changing in recent years. There was a time when most thought that if one was not "filled with the Holy Spirit" (exercising gifts), then one did not yet have the Spirit present in them. However, we must remember that we have a triune God who is three in one and whose personalities cannot be separated one from another. God and Jesus cannot come into one's life in a rebirth experience without the Holy Spirit as part of that event.

What is often called the "baptism of the Holy Spirit" is merely a further release of the Holy Spirit who is already present so that the Spirit can operate with power within the believer. A charismatic is one who understands and allows the spiritual gifts to be released within his life. Spiritual gifts are given to equip the individual Christian for ministry and for the edification of the body of Christ.

Pentecostal refers to those old-line charismatics who first came into the "fullness of the Spirit." Generally, it refers to people who are more emotionally demonstrative and who probably will profess the doctrine that if you haven't spoken in tongues, you don't "have" the Spirit. Pentecostals tend to think of the Holy Spirit as working upon a person to cause the person to act in ways that he or she would not ordinarily act.

Too often, old-line Pentecostals are those who may have spoken in tongues only once. They tend to think that speaking in tongues is something that happens to you, and they never really understand that one who has the gift of tongues can speak in tongues any time he or she wants.

> If anyone speaks in a tongue, two—or at the most three—should speak, one at a time, and someone must interpret.
>
> —1 CORINTHIANS 14:27

In contrast, a truly charismatic person understands incarnation—that the Holy Spirit works in and through one's natural personality and giftedness. Ideally, charismatic Christians understand that we hold our gifts in earthen vessels and that we are responsible for the way in which those gifts are exercised.

Speaking in tongues is a form of speaking and/or singing praises to God in the Spirit. It is a devotional prayer to the Lord that circumvents the limiting filters of our mind.

In the one who employs the private gift of speaking or singing in tongues, the Holy Spirit empowers him or her to sing with one's spirit to God's Spirit for the purpose of praise and to be refreshed spiritually. This form of tongues is between the individual and God and requires no interpretation. Its primary value in equipping one for ministry is in the spiritual refreshment it produces for the one caught up in pure spirit-to-Spirit worship.

Interpretation of tongues is only necessary when the direction of communication is reversed and God gives a message for the body of Christ through the one speaking in tongues. This calls for someone to interpret to others what God may be saying. That is, one who is equipped with the gift of interpretation communicates the message from God in a known tongue so the church may be edified.

Can a charismatic person, exercising his spiritual gifts, have a slumbering personal spirit? Would not the releasing of the Holy Spirit's power in one's life tend to awaken the personal spirit?

Not necessarily so! It is almost never that the Holy Spirit alone awakens a person's personal spirit. This is because ours is an incarnational faith, and Jesus wants the church to be involved in this happening. Person to person, Jesus wants people to love each other to life.

Spiritual gifts refer to the special empowerment given by God through the Holy Spirit to each individual, equipping a person to do God's work in the world for the edification of the church.

We have not been given a definitive list of spiritual gifts in the New Testament, but they are enumerated in the context of several of Paul's letters to the early churches. Depending on how one interprets his applications, the spiritual gifts include the following:

Gift	Description	Scripture
Administra-tion	Ability to efficiently orga-nize people and resources to accomplish God's specific goals	1 Cor. 12:28

Gift	Description	Scripture
Apostleship	Ability to inspire, found, and shape movements, or to transcend cross-cultural differences for missionary purposes to found churches	1 Cor. 12:28
Discernment	Capacity to differentiate truth from error or whether teachings are from God, man, or Satan, or ability to discern the presence of demons in or influencing people	1 Cor. 12:10
Evangelism	Desire and capacity to effectively share the gospel with others and lead them into saving faith in Christ	Eph. 4:11; Acts 21:8
Exhortation	Gift of counseling and encouraging others to become all that God wants them to be	Rom. 12:8
Faith	Ability to see God's purpose and to trust His wisdom and power to accomplish what seems impossible	1 Cor. 12:9
Giving	Willingness and ability to contribute eagerly and generously to the Lord's work	Rom. 12:8
Healing and miracles	Ability to be an instrument of God's power to accomplish spiritual and physical healing and other miracles	1 Cor. 12:9–10

Gift	Description	Scripture
Hospitality	Desire and talent to graciously share fellowship, food, and lodging in one's home	1 Pet. 4:9
Interpre- tation of tongues	Ability to interpret in a known language a message received from God through tongues speech	1 Cor. 12:10
Knowledge	Ability to know facts unaided by any means other than spiritual revelation	1 Cor. 12:8
Leadership	Ability to clearly see what must be done to accomplish God's work and to inspire others to cooperatively join in the task	Rom. 12:8
Mercy	Cheerful performance of ministry to others who are sick, hurting, or in crisis	Rom. 12:8
Music	Ability to communicate God's love and one's personal testi- mony through music	1 Cor. 14:15, 26
Prophecy	Ability to understand and communicate a word given directly from God	1 Cor. 12:10
Service	Gift of recognizing special needs and meeting them by giving of oneself joyfully and efficiently	1 Cor. 12:28; Rom. 12:7

Gift	Description	Scripture
Shepherding	Pastoral gift to guide, nurture, comfort, and protect a group of believers	Eph. 4:11; 1 Pet. 5:1–3
Speaking in tongues	Ability to praise God in the spirit or to receive messages from God, Spirit to spirit	1 Cor. 12:10
Teaching	Unusual facility to grasp and communicate God's truth so others can clearly understand	1 Cor. 12:28; Rom. 12:7
Wisdom	Divine insight of how to apply biblical principles to different issues in life	1 Cor. 12:8

It is a common misunderstanding among many evangelical church people that to be charismatic is to speak in tongues. Or to put it another way, if you do not speak in tongues, you are not a charismatic Christian. But this is not so. If you recognize and use the spiritual gifts within you, whatever they may be, then you are indeed Spirit-filled and may be considered charismatic.

One who exercises several gifts of the Spirit is not necessarily more spiritual or more Christian than one who uses only one gift. This is the point Paul communicated so forcefully in 1 Corinthians 12 and 13. Pride has no place among those who exercise the Holy Spirit's gifts. Each person's gifts are but tools for ministry, and all gifts are necessary for the body of Christ to function—just as all members of the human body are necessary for it to function. The issue of tongues or any other gift should never be held up as a measure of how spiritual one is or whether one is truly a Spirit-filled Christian.

Fruit of the Spirit refer to attitudes and actions that result from the presence of the Holy Spirit in the Christian's life. In Galatians 5:22–23, Paul speaks of love, joy, peace, patience, kindness, goodness, faithfulness, gentleness, and self-control.

For purposes of remembering the distinction between spiritual gifts and fruit of the Spirit, we can say that *gifts* refer to the supernatural endowments used in serving the Lord, whereas *fruit* refer to the loving attitude and ethical actions shown by the servant. We tend to think of someone exercising dramatic gifts as being "really Christian." However, we can see true Christianity by observing the fruit of the Spirit—a father lovingly hugging his children, a mother joyously giving of herself in patient nurture, someone sticking by a troubled friend with kind acceptance and love, or one controlling the temptation to sin.

> *Lord,*
>
> *I want to be fully awakened—set free to be transformed by Your power into the glory of Your likeness. I long for a rich and satisfying relationship with You and the fulfillment of all that You created me to be.*
>
> *By Your grace, Lord, enable me to forgive those who were unable to nurture me to life.*

Forgive me for all the ways I have withdrawn from intimacy and held bitterness and negative expectations in my heart. Forgive me for striving to win love and acceptance without the willingness or ability to hold my heart open to others.

Melt my heart of stone, Lord. Fill me with life and give me strength of spirit to persist in risking to choose life. Enable me to be vulnerable to people through whom You would give me nurture of mind, body, soul, and spirit.

Set me free from slumber, and empower me to bring life and joy to others. Amen.

CHAPTER 1 AWAKENING EXERCISES

1. In your own words, write a brief definition of each of these terms:

   Personal spirit

   _____

   _____

   Soul

   _____

   _____

   Mind

   _____

   _____

   Body

   _____

   _____

   To reinforce your understanding, explain each of these terms to a friend or to fellow group members. Discuss your definitions and answer questions, but avoid getting into disputes over disagreement about terms.

2. What is an evangelical Christian? What must happen in the life of an evangelical Christian for one to be considered a charismatic?

_____

_____

_____

3. What is a spiritual gift? For what purpose are spiritual gifts given?

_____

_____

_____

4. Review the list of spiritual gifts mentioned in this chapter. Which of these are you aware of in your own life? Ask others to reveal to you what gifts they believe you have been given.

_____

_____

5. In your own words, write what is meant by "fruit of the Spirit."

_____

_____

6. Explain how one might be filled with the Holy Spirit and be exercising spiritual gifts yet not be showing fruit of the Spirit. If you can, give an example from your own life.

    _____

    _____

7. Memorize the nine fruit of the Spirit enumerated in Galatians 5:22–23. For each, write down a specific way you might attempt to exemplify spiritual fruit in your relationships with others. Keep this list as a daily reminder to be more aware of how your Christian faith can make a difference in your attitude and behavior.

    Love _____

    Joy _____

    Peace _____

    Patience _____

    Kindness _____

    Goodness _____

    Faithfulness _____

    Gentleness _____

    Self-control _____

2

WHAT CAUSES THE
SPIRIT TO SLUMBER?

WHEN WE PUT THIS QUESTION TO THE LORD IN prayer, He revealed to us that when a person slumbers in the spirit, it is a result of not coming into one's full humanity. We are used to dealing with a variety of definitions for *human being*, as put forth by the disciplines of anthropology, sociology, psychology, or philosophy, but God has provided a distinctly different definition.

Essentially, to be human is to have an awakened personal spirit by which one identifies and empathizes with others, becomes one with them, and cherishes what is in the other person even more than one's own life.

> Greater love has no one than this, that he lay down his life for his friends.
>
> —JOHN 15:13

> Each of you should look not only to your own interests, but also to the interests of others.
>
> —PHILIPPIANS 2:4

An even shorter way to define what it is to be fully human would be to say one word—*Jesus.* Jesus, as the second Adam, is our example of what God intended for His human creation. Yes, man is a fallen creature. We all have sinned and fall short of God's ideal, but it is God's desire that we be saved from our sin and be restored to a right relationship with Him. That is the fullness of humanity for which we were created. Jesus came to Earth as God incarnate to be the means for our salvation. As we give ourselves in faith to live in Jesus Christ and He lives in us, we are transformed into His image. Thus we become more human.

UNDERSTANDING OUR HUMANNESS

We get things backward when we say, "Oh, I did that wrong thing because I am only human." We should call our hurtful, unethical, and immoral ways our *inhumanity* because such behavior is the result of our unredeemed selves.

When we consider the ideal of human nature (man as his best self), we are not talking about what is known as humanism. Humanism is the glorification of the human position—putting man at the center of his universe. Humanism is Satan's copy of what God is doing to transform men and women into the character of Jesus Christ through His saving grace.

Ours is an incarnational faith. Scripture tells us, "The Word became flesh" (John 1:14). The Word didn't just visit in flesh; it *became* flesh so that we could identify with our Creator and commune with Him spirit to Spirit. We do not have bodies in which our spirits slosh around like water in a glass, from which one day the spirit will go back to heaven. Each of us is one being—mind, spirit, and body—flowing together. Through the spirit (the life force) breathed into us by God, we are to become human beings, sanctified by God's grace and growing in relationship with Him.

But we humans don't become human just by being born. We have to be nurtured into becoming human. The human is dependent upon his mother and father longer than any species in all of creation. We are not societal by accident; it is by necessity.

The need for affection

There are certain kinds of nurture needed for us to grow in our humanness. The first of these is affection. We do not become human beings unless we experience affectionate touch—as babies, toddlers, children growing up, teenagers, and adults. We do not retain our humanity without continuing to touch others with clean, wholesome love and affection.

Touch imparts life and energy. Touch imparts security and strength. Touch communicates the vital element of meeting spirit to spirit with another person. We have to be held to properly develop our true humanity.

Here is the crucial lesson that much of the world has yet to discover. It is extremely difficult to become human beings with fully awakened personal spirits without nurture in the context of the family—from father and mother, grandparents, siblings, and other relatives.

Fathers are extremely important in this process. They are primary in the awakening of the personal spirits of infants and children. This is not to denigrate mothers or to undervalue their importance in giving love and care and all kinds of nurture to the child, but fathers were created to fulfill a special role. They have a developmental task to call their children into life as functioning spirits.

> And, ye fathers, provoke not your children to wrath: but bring them up in the *nurture* and admonition of the Lord.
>
> —EPHESIANS 6:4, KJV, EMPHASIS ADDED

When a baby is conceived, the child needs the father's spirit near the mother, feeling the father's presence even while in the womb. The newborn baby needs to be held by the father, to be comforted in the night, to be burped, to be given dry diapers, and to be sung lullabies. This role of the father is critical. A newborn baby is familiar with his mother's womb, but outside the womb the baby learns for the first time how to meet another person through the personal spirit. The baby is drawn forth and taught how to function not only by the mother's nurture but also by the father's nurture.

Ideally, the father should be the first person who is primary to the child outside the womb to give nurture through affectionate touch. This is a different kind of strength than that which comes through physical bonding with the mother. The baby's personal spirit flows out into the father and drinks from the father's spirit. The baby blesses the father, and the father returns the blessing through loving presence and touch. The baby learns in the spirit how to meet a person other than its mother. The importance of this cannot be overemphasized.

Listen to the Scriptures. The prophet Malachi describes the great day of the coming of the Lord Almighty, when the people must respond to the laws of God or suffer the consequences.

> See, I will send you the prophet Elijah before that great and dreadful day of the LORD comes. He will turn the hearts of the fathers to their children, and the hearts of the children to their fathers; or else I will come and strike the land with a curse.
>
> —MALACHI 4:5–6

The Hebrew culture of the Old Testament was a tribal, patriarchal society in which the father was clearly identified as the head of the family. That role and its subsequent expectations were clearly understood. Malachi might well have said that the hearts of parents must turn to their children and the children to their parents. Or he might well have said that families should be families and their members should take care to nurture one another. Those things are also true. But the message is clear that the father is expected to assume the leadership role. In the purpose of God, fathers are primary in teaching their children's personal spirits how to function.

The need for loving discipline

The father's responsibility also is to provide the child with admonishment and discipline. Fathers should define limits to their children in respect to how they relate to others in their personal spirits. Fathers should take seriously the task of being strong and firm when needed to say to the child, "This is where you stop. I am not letting you run amok."

> Folly is bound up in the heart of a child, but the rod of discipline will drive it far from him.
>
> —PROVERBS 22:15

Strong, thoughtful, and loving leadership on the part of the father can create a family environment in which authority is respected, boundaries are understood, communication remains open, and parents can work together to provide discipline the child needs to thrive in the spirit. If the father is not there to provide that very important leadership and personal involvement, a part of the child's spirit withers and falls asleep. This inevitably results in a stunting of emotional and spiritual growth.

The need for strong family structures

Let's consider historically and culturally what is happening in our nation. In Malachi 4:5–6, the prophet spoke of the need for the hearts of fathers to turn to their children and the hearts of the children to their fathers, "or else I will come and strike the land with a curse."

That curse is unfolding for us right now. We are living out the consequences of not following the admonition of God for fathers to assume proper family leadership and for family members to turn to each other in the process of nurturing their personal spirits.

Before World War I, the nuclear family (father, mother, and children) was a more cohesive unit. Most people lived in the context of an extended family—grandparents, aunts, uncles, and cousins. Society was much less mobile than it is today. People tended to live for longer periods of time in geographical proximity to those they grew up with; they tended to spend more time together, and they knew each other more intimately.

It was also a more affectionate age, even in the way people expressed themselves. Have you ever read letters written during that period of history? We would think of them today as almost corny. "O my dear soul, without you the sun does not rise; I do not see the moon. You are my very life..." It was a mushy, but affectionate age.

During the First World War, when fathers went overseas and were gone for long periods of time, there was still an extended family left behind to fill in the role of the father for young children. There were grandfathers and uncles who spent time with the children, held them affectionately, and nurtured them. Consequently, more people grew up having awakened personal spirits and a heightened sense of true conscience. They were more capable of sustaining relationships, and families tended to stay together.

But after the war, the entire nation became more mobile. Mass production of inexpensive automobiles enabled more people to have better transportation. Families were able to travel greater distances, and members of the extended family lived farther apart than was previously practical. Increased industrialization brought more people to the cities from rural areas.

The crash of the stock market and the Great Depression that followed also tended to disintegrate many families and create even greater mobility. Hundreds of thousands of people migrated to other parts of the nation, seeking better employment opportunities.

Then came World War II. Fathers again went off to war, mothers went to work in war plants, and children grew up in child-care centers or in the care of friends. It was not an uncommon experience for men to be away two or three years and come home to toddlers who had never known them. An entire generation of young children missed out on the essential kind of fatherly nurturing they needed in the earliest years to provide them with fully awakened personal spirits.

The Korean War soon followed, and not too many years later, the Vietnam War. Millions of men again were away from their homes and their young children.

When troops came back from all these wars, they found themselves so psychologically wounded and so far behind in their education and careers that, in many cases, they just got their wives pregnant and went off to bury themselves in school or the workforce. Mothers were left to raise the kids. Or mothers also went to work or school, and grandparents or child-care centers were left to raise the kids.

Another entire generation of children made do without close relationships with their dads and/or other primary persons in their lives. The result has been a failure to receive the nurturing needed to sustain an awakened personal spirit.

The consequences we are seeing today are reflected in divorce rates. More than half of all marriages fail. Cohabitation without marriage has increased dramatically. The number of single-parent families has skyrocketed. Traditional standards of morality have severely eroded. Why?

> ❧ Communication on a deep personal level
> does not happen when one's spirit is
> slumbering.

- Long-term personal relationships cannot be sustained when one's spirit is slumbering.

- A true conscience cannot actively work in one's life to avoid trouble when the personal spirit is slumbering.

- Past experiences cannot wisely be remembered to prevent future mistakes when one's spirit is slumbering.

- A close personal relationship with God that will heal woundedness cannot be developed when one's spirit is slumbering.

Do you understand what is happening? Families are disintegrating, and generations of people with slumbering spirits are raising ensuing generations of slumbering spirits. The result is the curse of entire communities trying to live without adequate communication skills, without loving interpersonal relationships, without true conscience, and without respect for others and the logic of law and order.

Marian Wright Edelman, in her award-winning book *The Measure of Our Success*, expresses her belief that the greatest threat to our nation's security and future does not come from external enemies but from the enemy within—specifically "our loss of strong, moral, family, and community values and support."[1]

She confesses that, like so many parents, she worries about spending too much time and energy providing her children with opportunities and "things" she didn't have growing up, and also about shielding them from problems and barriers she faced as a black child and woman. She feels it is most important to clearly share the positive experiences she did have while growing up—family, community, and spiritual values that helped immunize her against the plagues of indifference, defeatism, negativism, selfishness, and hopelessness.

We are reaping the consequences of a poverty of nurture that has crippled the personal spirits of growing children.

Our nation is experiencing a crisis in moral values because moral values are not a part of the nurture and teaching in every home as they should be. For the first time in our nation's history, many communities cannot build a school without making it look like a prison. Schools have to be surrounded by fences, with limited access, guarded doors, and metal detectors. This is to keep students in for their own protection and to keep drug dealers, who with no conscience would prey on students, out. These drastic measures may also be to keep out the vandals who would come in and with no conscience rip up the classrooms. Specially trained guards have to patrol the school hallways to keep students from fighting or to confiscate guns and knives from those who do not know how to communicate except through threats and violence.

Because so many people have no respect for others and no conscience about wrongdoing, even times of celebration can break into drunken violence. We have seen this happen in the streets of several cities following championship wins of athletic teams. Hooliganism at games and public concerts has become common.

DEPRIVATION OF NURTURE

Why do we have this state of affairs? Because entire segments of our society have been so deprived of nurture in the home and have had little or no spiritual influence from their families, particularly from fathers. Consequently, they have closed themselves off, and their personal spirits are virtually dead.

A few years ago, we were speaking at an Episcopal church in the heart of Brooklyn, New York. As we were about to go out for lunch, the rector warned us that it was a very rough neighborhood and that we should stay in groups for our own safety. He made it clear that we should never go on the street alone at night. Otherwise, he said, you run the chance of being robbed, beaten, or even killed. Bands of youths have no conscience and no concern over doing harm to other people because there is little moral training in their homes. This condition is not limited to the streets of New York, Detroit, Chicago, or Los Angeles. Even in the prosperous suburbs of less-notorious cities, it is not uncommon to find adolescent gangs, random vandalism, and widespread drug use. A major contributing factor to these kinds of problems is that a lot of the children come from homes headed by single parents, or from second- or third-marriage homes with children who are "his, hers, and ours," with no clear sense of close-knit family unity.

Even children who have been nurtured with loving care in the stability of a strong home are not without the danger of slipping into spiritual slumber as adults. We live in a secular society, and it is easy to slide into patterns of superficiality and noninvolvement. We anesthetize the spirit through:

- Impersonality in the workplace and in the neighborhood

- Isolation from the natural extended family through distance or divorce

- Little or no involvement in personal devotions or in corporate worship through the church

- Busywork and recreational schedules that allow little time for relationship building and intimate conversation

- Casual attitudes toward sexual involvement outside of marriage

- Overexposure to violence, resulting in insensitivity to the hurts and feelings of others

Do you understand why there is so little concern for the rights and welfare of others, so much fragmentation in the family, so much divorce, and so much crime? The curse spoken of in Malachi 4:5–6 is of our own making.

The essential structures of love and discipline from parents and the extended family are sorely lacking. Even more specifically, fathers are not being fathers. When fathers do not nurture their children with affectionate touching and the steady hand of love and discipline, the personal spirits of children are jeopardized. What kind of world will we have if the continuing trend of spiritual slumber goes unchanged? We need only to look at Scripture to see a very clear catalog of qualities that will dominate our society. (Or is that time already here?)

> People will be lovers of themselves, lovers of money, boastful, proud, abusive, disobedient to their parents, ungrateful, unholy, without love, unforgiving, slanderous, without self-control, brutal, not lovers of the good, treacherous, rash, conceited, lovers of pleasure rather than lovers of God—having a form of godliness but denying its power.
>
> —2 TIMOTHY 3:2–5

Saint Paul is not speaking here of the world at large. He is speaking of those who are in the church—who "have a form of godliness" but deny its power. We cannot escape the curse of slumbering spirits just by being actively involved in the church. People with slumbering spirits can accept the plan of salvation mentally and yet relate only to law, theology, and doctrine rather than the person of Jesus. They don't meet Jesus on a personal level because their spirits are asleep.

People can get into a charismatic church and be caught up in the emotional excitement of raising their hands in praise and singing. But all too often if the Lord left the worship service, they wouldn't know the difference because they are only into the worship form. They don't know Jesus because their spirits are slumbering.

Others can get into a liturgical church and be emotionally moved by the rituals and symbols of the service (again, the worship form). But they don't know God because their spirits are asleep.

Slumbering in the spirit is the crux of what is wrong with many people today and the primary key of what has happened to infect the church with apathy.

Persons asleep in their spirit have brought on a crisis of conscience and a growing epidemic of callousness and immorality.

We must understand the nature of this condition if we are to understand why there is so little intimate communication between people, so little moral sensitivity, so much alienation, and so many fractured families. We face major problems that boil down to the need for the hearts of fathers and mothers to turn to their children with the kind of fully involved, loving, touching, and disciplined nurture that is essential to infuse vitality into the personal spirit.

LOOKING PAST PROBLEMS WITH HOPEFUL HEARTS

You may be wondering right now, "Well, good grief! My father never provided the kind of close and loving nurture described here. Who wouldn't react by closing their hearts? Now I don't know how to open it. Is there any hope for me?"

In thinking about this, don't panic or go into depression. As you become aware of the ways in which your spirit slumbers, you can begin to focus on how to overcome the stronghold your heart formed in reaction to that prior lack of nurture. What you will be doing will end your loneliness. You no longer will have to think that you are the only wounded soul in the church. Many others share in your condition.

As we come together, we can begin to love each other back to life.

As you read on, you will have opportunity to consider ten primary characteristics of an awakened spirit and the common characteristics of persons whose spirits are slumbering. These characteristics are laid out in chapters 3, 4, and 5. As you evaluate yourself, you probably will discover that your spirit is slumbering in several areas.

Because we are all in the same soup, we can also be in the same blessing. If you understand where you seem to be most asleep in your spirit, you can be more aware of how to compensate for that and how to seek healing through God's power and the love of Christian friends.

Heavenly Father,

Give me an understanding of what it means to be truly human—to walk each day in the steps of the Lord Jesus Christ, who is the model of love, goodness, and grace that You have set out as our guide.

Help me to live happily under the discipline of Your grace and in turn to discipline those entrusted to my charge with the steady hand of Your wisdom and unconditional love.

Help me to both give and receive affection with humility and purity of heart.

Help me to build strong and nurturing family structures, undergirded with reliance on You, our loving heavenly Father.

Help me to fix my sight on the Lord Jesus, who is that clear point of light with which You penetrate the wilderness of evil that surrounds us. Give me the strength and courage always to set my course straight for the light of His grace and restoring love. Amen.

Chapter 2 Awakening Exercises

1. Review what is written in this chapter about the way we use the words *human* and *inhumane*. What concept of human nature were you taught as a child? Have you grown up understanding humanness to be a high ideal or rather as a natural state of sin to be overcome?

   _____

   _____

   _____

   _____

   _____

2. Based on what you have learned in this chapter, write in your own words a new definition of what it means to be fully human.

   _____

   _____

   _____

   _____

   _____

3. This chapter lists three needs that must be fulfilled in order for one to maintain an awakened personal spirit: affection, loving discipline, and strong family structures. What is your personal story of how well these needs were met as you were growing up? (Share with a friend about the feelings you hold about each of these needs. Pray together about your feelings.)

_____

_____

_____

_____

_____

4. Read 2 Timothy 3:2–5. List ways in which Paul's description of those Christians might be a mirror of developing characteristics in your own life.

_____

_____

_____

_____

_____

5. If you could go back in time and create an environment in which to be renurtured in a more positive way, what would that experience be like? Share your description with a friend or in your small group. Ask the friend or small group to be a vessel through which God can supply nurture to you now.

_____

_____

_____

_____

_____

6. If you believe you need renurturing in order to wake your slumbering spirit, what sources of help can you think of? Who could contribute toward fulfilling that need? Make a list.

_____

_____

_____

_____

_____

PART II

CHARACTERISTICS OF AN AWAKENED PERSONAL SPIRIT

3

RELATING TO GOD

THE NEXT THREE CHAPTERS WILL EXPLORE TEN
ways an awakened personal spirit equips us to
function in our full humanity. We will also illustrate what happens when our spirits slumber in these areas.
When considering these ten characteristics of an awakened
personal spirit, be aware that no one is entirely asleep or
awake. Each person possesses his or her own distinctive spiritual makeup. Some will be more asleep than others. Some
may have areas in which they are fully awake while they are
woefully asleep in other areas. Some people may slip in and
out of sleepiness—being alert at times and then drifting off
into insensitivity.

As diagnostic tools in prayer ministry, we ask a series of questions to determine if a person's spirit is slumbering. Each of the ten sections dealing with characteristics of an awakened personal spirit will begin with a diagnostic question. Consider these carefully to help you get in touch with functions of your personal spirit most in need of awakening.

These characteristics of an awakened personal spirit have to do with:

Relating to God

1. Feeling God's presence in corporate worship
2. Feeling God's presence in private devotions
3. Experiencing real communication with God
4. Receiving inspiration from God

Relating to others

1. Transcending time to learn from past experiences
2. Communicating with others on a deep personal level
3. Sustaining long-term personal relationships
4. Experiencing the glory of Christian marital sex

Relating to oneself

1. Maintaining good health

2. Being guided by a true and working conscience

In this first chapter of this section we will begin with how an awakened spirit relates to God in public worship settings and in private devotions.

FEELING GOD'S PRESENCE IN CORPORATE WORSHIP

When you are in a worship service and others are joyously caught up in the preaching of the Word, singing, and praise, can you really feel God's presence, or do you just have to know by faith that He is there?

When God's Spirit moves within us in worship, He does not move just within our minds; He also moves within our personal spirits.

> Yet a time is coming and has now come when the true worshipers will worship the Father in spirit and truth, for they are the kind of worshipers the Father seeks. God is spirit, and his worshipers must worship in spirit and in truth.
>
> —JOHN 4:23–24

God quickens our spirits and enables us to worship. Listen to the Magnificat (the song of Mary). The King James translation helps us by its use of the tenses in which Mary spoke: "My soul doth magnify the Lord, and my spirit hath rejoiced in God my Saviour" (Luke 1:46–47, KJV).

Because Mary's spirit had rejoiced in God, she was quickened (caused to be enlivened or to be more sensitive and aware). This enabled the power of her spirit to flow out presently through her mind, character, and personality to magnify and worship the Lord.

> *Our personal spirits need to be strong enough to overcome the barriers self throws up against the abiding presence of God.*

A person who has an awakened personal spirit can come into a worship service and feel the presence of God's Holy Spirit flowing into the worshipers. This experience is apprehended differently by different persons, of course, depending upon the form of worship that is most uplifting to the individual.

It may come in the wonder of participation in Mass at a cathedral, in the singing of familiar hymns in a country church, or in the prayers and praise of a home fellowship of friends. The common element of the corporate worship experience is the feeling of being caught up into the presence of God. We praise God and sing to God, aided by the Holy Spirit. Worship happens when God comes and meets us and catches us up to Himself.

People who have slumbering spirits have difficulty getting from praise to worship because they are unable to experience the exhilarating feeling that should result when God's Spirit comes on them. Most of the time they will say, "I believe God is aware of our worship, but I have never really felt His presence in the way you are describing."

Such persons may sometimes feel God's presence as a flicker for a moment, but they are unable to stay and rest in His presence. Their personal spirit does not enable them to let go emotionally and enter fully into corporate worship. The result may be a wandering mind, visual distractions, inability to be comfortable with unfamiliar worship forms, preoccupation with one's problems, or even distrust or skepticism about what fellow worshipers are experiencing.

For whatever reason, God's abiding presence is not a reality because the person's spirit is not alive enough to let the glory of praise and worship overcome the barriers the self throws up. The spirit is numbed by slumber, and true worship in the presence of God seldom, if ever, happens.

FEELING GOD'S PRESENCE IN PRIVATE DEVOTIONS

During times of prayer and private devotions, can you feel God's presence lifting you up in a real way? A person having a fully awakened personal spirit will be able to individually and privately pray, read Scripture, and praise God with a real sense of the presence of the Lord Jesus Christ. This will be accompanied by feeling His glory all around, lifting you up, refreshing you, and equipping you for the day. Job 32:8 says, "But it is the spirit in a man, the breath of the Almighty, that gives him understanding."

This sense of spiritual presence does not happen when our personal spirit is slumbering. When asked about feeling God's presence in private devotions, a slumberer's characteristic reply might be, "No, I can't, but at least I can spend time in Bible study, and I make that a part of my devotions."

When our spirit is slumbering, even Bible study becomes an exercise in reading mere words. Have you ever had the experience of reading a book when you were distracted or your mind was wandering onto other things? Suddenly you realize you have read an entire paragraph without comprehending what you just read.

Personal devotions require ability to enjoy being alone, to be quiet, and to focus on prayer, inspirational thoughts, Scripture reading, praise, and quiet listening for God to speak.

That is a common experience for those who attempt to have personal devotions when their spirit is slumbering. The focus and feeling of Bible reading are lost. The words have little impact because you cannot receive the quickening breath of God to sensitize your understanding.

You cannot maintain an attitude of sustained prayer because of a wandering mind or inability to be open to communication with God. You run dry and the experience falls dead. When this happens, it is easy to give up trying to have a personal devotional time.

Personal devotions require ability to enjoy being alone, to be quiet, and to focus on prayer, inspirational thoughts, Scripture reading, praise, and quiet listening for God to speak. These are characteristics of the personal spirit that God is able to quicken into devotional sensitivity.

Do you find it uncomfortable to be alone, preferring always to have someone with you, to go shopping, to travel, to study, even to be entertained? Do you find it uncomfortable to experience silence, always wanting to have a radio or TV playing, or to be engaged in some kind of busy activity or conversation?

Some might protest that being alone or experiencing quiet moments is boring to them. But for the person with an awakened personal spirit, times alone or times of quiet solitude characteristically are stimulating and exciting times because the spirit can then soar, unimpeded by distractions or the demands of other people. It is in this environment that focused devotion can result in very rewarding times of worship and intimacy with the Lord.

Of course, personality types vary greatly. Some people are more introverted by nature and seem to draw energy and affirmation from within themselves. They tend to be more comfortable working alone or spending time by themselves. Other people have more extroverted personalities and draw their energy from outside themselves, getting stimulation, companionship, and affirmation in the presence of others.

However, in our experience of dealing with many different people with different personality types, those who have awakened personal spirits are growing toward more security in their inner being and can relax and focus in time spent alone. Even the extrovert can come to enjoy the silence. The spirit is able to let go and be aware of God's presence. The senses are heightened, and true worship becomes a reality.

EXPERIENCING REAL COMMUNICATION WITH GOD

Do you ever hear the voice of God? Do you ever have spiritual dreams or visions, or know in some other way with certainty what God is saying to you? Be honest now. Are you among the skeptics? When you hear someone say he hears the voice of God, is your first reaction that he is either psychotic or a religious charlatan? Unfortunately, that is the common reaction for most people in society today because listening to God is such an uncommon practice.

Indeed, there are people with mental illness who think they hear God but actually do not. There are dishonest religious manipulators who make questionable claims on what God asks of us in order to attract followers and make financial gain. And there are religious cult leaders who have disgraced the Christian church with wildly distorted teachings and ridiculous claims of messages from God that only serve their own perverse purposes. But there also is the reality of God directly communicating with those whose spirits are awake enough to hear Him. God guides and enriches those who listen to Him "in spirit and in truth" (John 4:24).

If one is not aware that God is attempting to communicate directly, it may be that the spirit to whom God is speaking is too numbed for the message to penetrate the mind.

A major part of hearing what is said to you is a result of paying attention. Particularly in our age of multimedia and multitasking, it is difficult to stay tuned in enough to hear even the audible messages that come our way.

If you have an active child involved in a distracting game, it is often necessary as a parent to get his attention by gently taking his face in your hands and saying firmly, "Now look at me, and pay attention to what I'm saying!" Sometimes it is helpful to ask that the message be repeated verbally to be certain it was properly understood.

God will seldom grab us by the face and make us listen, although sometimes a crisis in life may serve that purpose. Generally, listening to God takes practice. You have to pay attention, and you have to be aware of some of the subtle ways God communicates His will.

The ability to hear God communicate is heightened by an awakened spirit. If one is not aware that God is attempting to communicate directly, it may be that the spirit to whom

God is speaking is too numbed for the message to penetrate the mind.

The typical reply to the question we asked above is, "No. I guess I have to believe that those people who keep saying the Lord tells them things are not fooling themselves, but God never talks to me." Another typical reply might be, "I believe God answers prayers, but I don't think He speaks directly to people in ways they can actually hear."

People who have an awakened personal spirit know God often speaks through dreams, and they stand ready to listen. They may have dreams that come true or have distinct symbolic meanings that hold a message from God they can clearly understand. They also get pictures or visions in their minds that communicate a message. Sometimes they may even hear the voice of God speaking to their minds, as it were, or even audibly. God speaks from His Spirit to our spirit. But a spirit that is asleep cannot hear.

> As it is written: "No eye has seen, no ear has heard, no mind has conceived what God has prepared for those who love him"—but God has revealed it to us by his Spirit. The Spirit searches all things, even the deep things of God.
>
> —1 CORINTHIANS 2:9–10

RECEIVING INSPIRATION FROM GOD

Do you sense that it is God who inspires you with fresh ideas and creative ability? God wants to give us inspiration.

This inspiration is not just in the Christian context; it is the unleashing of creative insight and power in all areas of life.

- Envisioning creative ideas
- Building fresh and exciting new solutions
- Interpreting with sensitivity
- Simplifying the complex
- Clarifying the obscure
- Integrating the diverse
- Expressing with power
- Leading with charisma

Have you ever known someone who has studied poetry and knows meter, scanning, imagery, and all the literary forms, and yet what he writes is doggerel? The message is pedantic, the imagery is flat, and the words have no life or power. What is lacking is inspiration.

On the other hand, someone else may not even be a serious student of poetry; yet when you read what he or she writes, it practically jumps off the page. The poetry has internal rhythm, powerful imagery, and sensitivity of expression that captures your imagination and moves you emotionally. It is inspired.

Similarly, a person may study painting and understand line, shape, value, symmetry, color theory, and all the other principles of visual art. But when you look at his painting, it leaves you flat. It is nothing but technique, and it lacks feeling. Another painter may apply a few simple brush strokes, and you look at it with wonder. Even in the simplicity, there is power and something creatively unique. What is the difference? One has inspiration added to discipline; the other does not.

Inspiration and creativity flows easily when your spirit is open to the possibility of new ideas and unexplored territories. It is more about spiritual openness than religion.

We have an engineer friend who characterizes the co-workers in his office as fitting two basic categories: drones and innovators. Drones are engineers who primarily apply the common solutions that other people have already worked out. Drones seldom get an original idea. Their thinking is very practical but also very flat. They lack inspiration to come up with innovative solutions.

On the other hand, he sees some engineers as being very creative innovators. They get all kinds of ideas and are excited by the challenge of finding new and efficient ways to solve engineering problems. The difference is in their ability to integrate their knowledge, logic, and exposure to new ideas into inspired thinking. There is a creative spark that is ignited by an awakened personal spirit.

It must be noted here that everyone has a personal spirit and God's inspiration can flow to believers and nonbelievers alike. In fact, religiously neutral persons may be better equipped to receive creative inspiration. Creativity flows more easily when your spirit is open to the possibility of new ideas and you freely risk the dangers of striking out into unexplored territories. Such creativity requires a kind of singular focus for inspiration to truly take root. In this sense, an awakened personal spirit has less to do with religion than with spiritual openness.

In addition, inspiration can come more often and more readily to the young at heart who can deal with life from a simpler point of view and be open to a wider range of possibilities. Thomas Hart Benton, perhaps the most influential American mural painter in the twentieth century, was known for the wonderful simplicity of his images portraying the indomitable spirit of man. He was an active artist, painting well into his eighties. From gazing at his work, you can see the vibrancy of life permeating from the paintings. It is obvious that he valued young, hard-working people and that they too were capable of dealing with the fresh ideas that so stimulated him.

One's Christian belief and commitment may or may not be a factor in how awakened the personal spirit is to receive gifts from God. This is especially true in the area of creative inspiration. It would be wonderful to experience one's Christian faith enhancing creative capacity, as has been the case with many artists, writers, scientists, and world leaders throughout history. However, oftentimes the Christian believer is so locked up in restricting forms of religion that his spirit is given little chance to soar. Or one may be so burdened with the responsibilities of family care or of ministry that his spirit is not free enough to recognize inspiration from God or to fly with it when it comes.

God pours out inspiration to every awakened spirit capable of receiving it. Wonderful harmony can result in a life when God's inspiration flows into the awakened personal spirit of a Spirit-filled Christian. But we must recognize too that God's inspiration flows into the awakened spirits of nonbelievers as well and that they often produce wonderfully creative works of art, music, literature, and scientific invention.

Lord,

I pray that my spirit might be awakened to fully experience awe and wonder at the beauty of Your creation. Kindle a light inside me so I may appreciate the dazzling color of the evening sky, the graceful dancing of wheat fields caressed by the breeze, and the tender affection in the eyes of a loved one.

Open my ears to the music of a child's laughter, the exciting sound of a ball cracking against a bat, and the pleasant swish of under-brush as I walk a path on my way to a fishing stream.

Inspire my mind and move my hands to partake of Your wonderful, creative Spirit. Let me be refreshed and lifted by Your presence, comfortable with You even in silence, sensi-

tive to Your direction, and comforted by Your Spirit.

And, Lord, make me a vessel to catch Your good gifts of inspiration with excitement so that I might share them with holy and considerate zeal. Amen.

CHAPTER 3 AWAKENING EXERCISES

1. Review the four characteristics of an awakened personal spirit listed in this chapter. Rate yourself on a scale of 1 to 5 (1 = least awake, 5 = most awake) by circling the degree to which you feel your spirit is awake in each characteristic.

    Feel God's presence in corporate worship

1	2	3	4	5

    Feel God's presence in private devotion

1	2	3	4	5

    Aware of God communicating with you

1	2	3	4	5

    Receiving inspiration from God

1	2	3	4	5

2. If you have difficulty experiencing God's presence in corporate worship, can you identify what distracts you? On a sheet of paper, draw a line down the middle from top to bottom. On the left side, make a list of things that commonly distract you during worship. On the right, jot down ways in which you might lessen those distractions to become more focused on personally relating to God.

3. If you have difficulty feeling God's presence in private devotions, try these simple exercises to encourage a more frequent and more focused devotional life:

⇔| Pray flash prayers frequently throughout the day. Make them simple, eyes-open conversations with God to ask for help, to request His uplifting presence, or to thank and praise Him. Try to develop an active attitude of prayer.

⇔| To shut out visual distractions during your time of private devotions, light a candle in a darkened, quiet room. Focus your attention on the flame to help you concentrate on the presence of God's Holy Spirit. Pray aloud to God about whatever comes to mind. Be honest and confessional without trying to be eloquent.

⇔| Listen to gospel music with earphones. Darken the room or close your eyes to shut out distractions. Listen carefully to the meaning of the words. If you prefer, listen to classical music. Imagine your entire body being bathed in the presence of the Holy Spirit.

4. If direct communication from God seems to be something very distant from you, begin by accepting in faith that it can and will happen if you allow yourself to be open enough. Create an environment in which you can

pay close attention to the ways God may be speaking to you.

- ⇥ Read the Beatitudes from the fifth chapter of Matthew by candlelight. Do not read just to get finished. Pause with each verse and ponder its meaning. Pray for God to reveal a special message to you from each passage. Take time to listen for an answer. God may speak through your own thoughts, especially if they come into consciousness easily and restfully.

- ⇥ Sit on the beach and watch the waves come in, or go into the woods and quietly observe nature all around you. Think carefully about what you are experiencing. Is God unfolding symbolic messages to you as you experience the wonders of nature?

- ⇥ Do you have recurring dreams? Keep a pad and pen by your bed. As soon as you wake up, think back through your dream and then jot down what you dreamed before you forget. Discuss your dreams with a Christian friend, and consider ways God may be communicating with you through them. Dreams are usually more symbolic than literal. Look for the messages within the symbols.

5. Pray for God's inspiration to make you a more creative and innovative person. Ask God to help you see ordinary things in new and creative ways. Pay attention when you get a fresh idea. Say, "Thank You, God!" Then use the idea by sharing it with others. Build on your new discoveries with a grateful heart.

4

RELATING TO
OTHERS

D O LESSONS OF THE PAST GRIP YOU WITH sufficient power to keep you from committing the same sins again? Or do your memories fade? Do future possibilities excite you enough to energize you to stick it out through problems and help you make good decisions? Or do you feel stuck in the present moment?

The ability to learn from the past and to project into the future is what we call "transcending time." It is the ability to connect what was, what is, and what can be.

For example: a couple comes in to see us for prayer ministry. They have awakened personal spirits, but they have some trouble spots in their marriage that will require hard work from both of them. Because their spirits are awake, they have the ability to remember good things in their marriage. They can also project into the future that once they get past their present trouble, their relationship can be restored to a healthy state. Their spirits enable them to connect what was, what is, and what can be with power to effect their emotions and create hope. They can make sense of the cause-and-effect relationships required to get them from where they are to where they want to go.

On the other hand, another couple comes in for prayer ministry, but they have no ability to remember the good things of the past with any compelling sense of reality. They have no ability to project into the future a belief that a good relationship can be restored. They are trapped in the present. They can't transcend the present moment and can only focus on their current hurts, quarrels, and unhappiness. Their slumbering spirits have made them dysfunctional and ill equipped to salvage their relationship and their marriage.

The young man mentioned previously, who had trouble paying his bills, had a slumbering spirit that kept him from transcending time. He could focus only on the present moment. When he saw something he liked, he would buy it right then in his excitement. If he didn't have the money, he would charge it with no thought to how he would have to pay for it later. By the time the creditors began calling, his memory of the purchase was so far removed that it had no reality to him. He saw the bill collectors only as a nuisance invading his present moment.

Have you ever been to a church service and experienced a powerful sermon in which the pastor warned, as Saint Paul did, that we all will be accountable for our deeds before the Lord? When someone goes out after hearing such a sermon and sins as though no Judgment Day is coming, you wonder, "How could he do that?"

Why? Because preaching to a person with a slumbering spirit about Judgment Day coming is like putting a quarter into a broken vending machine. It falls through and is rejected; there is no mechanism to catch the message. His spirit is slumbering. Neither the future nor the past has any compelling reality. The present moment cannot be transcended.

COMMUNICATING WITH OTHERS ON A DEEP PERSONAL LEVEL

In conversations, do you often sense what the other person is feeling so that you understand the meaning even before the words have been fully spoken? Or do you just have to figure out with your mind what others are trying to say?

It is a wonderfully refreshing feeling to be in conversation with someone when your spirits just seem to latch on to each other. When that happens, you become so tuned in to each other that you can leapfrog your thoughts. You don't even have to finish a sentence before the other person understands your meaning. You not only hear the words, but you also correctly sense the intent and the feeling of the conversation. That kind of communication is exciting and very fulfilling.

On the other hand, have you ever been in conversation with someone, thinking he or she was tracking with you, when unexpectedly the person says something that comes clear out of left field? You think, "Where did that come from? I thought we were tuned in to each other."

 Intimacy requires presence and a willingness to be self-revealing.

When this happens, it probably means that your conversational partner was following you with his mind rather than with his spirit. In order to communicate with you, he had to figure out with his mind how to respond. When the conversation took a curve, his mind couldn't follow. He just lost his focus and missed you altogether.

Good communication is essential for the intimacy level that should exist between close personal friends, within family groups, and between husband and wife. The kind of communication we are referring to here is much more than the ability to make interesting conversation. Interesting talk can happen without revealing yourself on a personal-feeling level.

When a man and woman commit themselves in a bond of marriage, there should be a developing intimacy level in which they can really come to understand and to know each other from their hearts. Spirit-to-spirit communication between persons results in being able to read each other's facial expressions or eyes, and especially to be able to sense emotional states without words being spoken. It results in appropriateness of response and behavior so that one does not violate the other person's feelings with impulsiveness or misunderstandings.

This kind of intimate communication can develop in various ways: through self-revealing talk, shared experiences, body language, sexual union, and the subtle communications of the spirit.

Building intimate relationships requires presence, and quality of presence is measured in terms of the self-revelation of meeting each other spirit to spirit. If the spirit is dysfunctional in a slumbering state, communication on a deep personal level cannot happen.

To evaluate your own awareness of how awake your spirit is in this area, consider these questions:

- Do you have several personal friends you share with regularly?

- When you talk with a person, can you comfortably maintain eye contact and stay focused on the conversation?

- How comfortable are you in sharing with your friends about the most personal things in your life?

⇥ How well do you think you know your spouse? Are you able to express feelings clearly, or do you frequently miscommunicate or choose not to really communicate at all?

⇥ How sensitive are you in understanding your spouse's needs, motives, responses, and heartfelt concerns? Ask your spouse to help you answer this question.

SUSTAINING LONG-TERM PERSONAL RELATIONSHIPS

Do you have a number of close relationships that, through good times and bad, have remained strong over a period of many years?

Family structures have become so fragmented and the self-concept of many people has become so confused that we are producing more and more slumbering spirits with each generation. When two people with slumbering spirits marry and have children, their children are likely to be asleep in their spirits as well. As a result, we wind up having generation after generation of families who develop serious dysfunctions.

When there is poor communication, relationships break down.

Inability to communicate adequately is a major cause of problems among family members. When two people with slumbering spirits get together, it is very difficult for them to tune in to each other. When they talk, it is as though an invisible wall surrounds them. This prevents real hearing, and their spirits do not mesh. Consequently, they remain isolated and alone, confined to superficial chatter. Their conversation is limited to the surface meaning of each other's words, while they miss the real feeling and intention behind what is being said. Because their spirits do not meet, they can't sense what the other person wants and needs. This results in inappropriate responses that subsequently make each partner feel isolated and lonely.

Such persons wind up being tremendously lonely. They can't hear the spirits of others, and they haven't learned to really talk from their own personal spirits. They just shadowbox about issues, reaching out only with their minds to grasp others.

It is no wonder that with such poor communication, relationships soon break down. When the personal spirit slumbers and communication is so difficult, frustration and loneliness set in. A couple may live together and yet remain in spiritual isolation in a dying relationship.

Long-term friendships and marriages are built between people who can engage each other's spirits and who can listen and talk on deep and intimate levels. Relationships are sustained by people who can talk out their differences, flex and bend, and grow stronger together because of what they have shared. Communication that builds and sustains relationships is one of the most important functions of the personal spirit.

 Relationships are sustained by people who can talk out their differences.

For the prayer minister, such communication capacity is the most important function. If you are involved in ministry, you must be able to tune in and feel with the other person so that what you say is appropriate to where the person is. If you cease to be appropriate, you violate the person with any insight you may have because you say it at the wrong time, at the wrong place, and in the wrong way. Your spirit must be awake to really listen, and it must be open to care about what is being said and what is not being said.

EXPERIENCING THE GLORY OF CHRISTIAN MARITAL SEX

Are the sexual relations in your marriage deeply fulfilling, intimate, spiritual experiences that cause you to cherish only your spouse as a sexual partner? If you are not already aware of this, we want to confirm to you that there is a special glory to Christian marital sex. The glory depends on the Holy Spirit singing through the wife's spirit, through every cell of her body, into the husband to tell him who he is. The glory depends on the Holy Spirit singing through the husband's spirit, through every cell of his body, into the wife to bless and fulfill her.

We want you to hear this as carefully as it can be said. There can never be glory of this kind in sex outside of marriage. It doesn't matter how much the man thinks he is in love with the woman and she with him, or how well they communicate. It absolutely cannot be because the Holy Spirit will not sing in immoral places. We need to get that clear.

A man may say he has had better sex with a woman other than his wife. Of course that may be true if he and his sex partner have been opening their hearts to one another and he hasn't been doing that with his wife. But good sex and the glory of sex are altogether different. The glory does not come except through the Holy Spirit singing through the husband and wife to each other, and this is an experience that only comes with an awakened spirit. Take a good look at the fifth chapter of Proverbs:

> Drink water from your own cistern,
> And fresh water from your own well.
> Should your springs be dispersed abroad,
> Streams of water in the streets?
> Let them be yours alone,
> And not for strangers with you.
> Let your fountain be blessed,
> And rejoice in the wife of your youth.
> As a loving hind and a graceful doe,
> Let her breasts satisfy you at all times;

Be exhilarated always with her love.
For why should you, my son, be exhilarated with an
   adulteress,
And embrace the bosom of a foreigner?

—PROVERBS 5:15–20, NAS

Husbands, your wife is the fountain God has given you. She is your drink of water. Her spirit is there to refresh you. Women have what our son Loren loves to call "chest power." It doesn't depend on the size of the breasts. It depends on the flow of the spirit. Power flows from the woman's breasts. It is a power to refresh the man.

As a pastor and prayer minister, I (John) sometimes come home from ministering to other people feeling completely exhausted. Even more than exhausted, it feels as though I have poured myself out until there is not a drop of humanity left in me. I lose the capability to be human with the kids. I feel like I am just dying inside. I need to be touched. In such a state, if my wife, Paula, comes at me with a lot of talk, she will miss me. But if she comes and puts her chest against me, I can feel her spirit flowing into me. This lines me up again, tells me who I am, and refills me with joy and vivacity.

Of course, the Holy Spirit of God is the first source of refreshment, but the Holy Spirit decides most often to refresh humanly through our spouses. That's the way He wants to do it. Women, when your husband comes home, don't come at him with a lot of talking. Put your chest up against him and hold on. You just let him think that you need it, but he needs it as much or more than you do.

To be earthy and practical here as well, we always say to young couples in marriage that pajamas are a great thing to hang on the bedposts in case of fire. Clothes insulate the flow of the electricity of your personal spirit. So our advice to married couples is to spend quiet time lying close together with the woman's chest against the man's. Let your spirits sing into each other and bring refreshment.

If you really experience the glory of Christian marital sex, you'll find that it is so good, so clean, so holy, so exhilarating that it will take your breath away. That kind of glory is the best deterrent to immorality. Scripture speaks clearly to the foolishness of adultery.

> But a man who commits adultery lacks judgment; whoever does so destroys himself.
>
> —Proverbs 6:32

> For out of the heart come evil thoughts, murder, adultery, sexual immorality, theft, false testimony, slander.
>
> —Matthew 15:19

> Flee from sexual immorality. All other sins a man commits are outside his body, but he who sins sexually sins against his own body. Do you not know that your body is a temple of the Holy Spirit, who is in you, whom you have received from God?
>
> —1 Corinthians 6:18–19

To commit adultery is to cause your extramarital sexual partner to tell you a lie about yourself. It confuses the issue of who you are and whom you belong to. Saint Paul explains in 1 Corinthians 6:16 that the act of joining yourself to a person sexually unites you with that person. You become "one with her in body," which leads to becoming "one flesh." The term "one flesh" is derived from Genesis 2:23:" This is now bone of my bones and flesh of my flesh." This speaks of the permanent union between Adam and Eve. "One flesh" does not mean only a physical union of two bodies; such a union remains permanently. Therefore it involves the whole person—heart, mind, soul, and spirit. When you have been united to more than one person in sexual unions, it fragments your spirit, it divides you against yourself, it betrays the holiness of your marriage relationship, and it defiles the sanctity of your body as the dwelling place of God's Holy Spirit. This is a heavy price to pay to satisfy lust.

Adultery confuses the issue of who you are and who you belong to.

Unfortunately, many people have bought the lie that it does not matter what you do with your body. "After all," they say, "what harm does it do to rub your body against another person as long as it is between two consenting adults?" This is the thinking of an underdeveloped conscience—the insensitive rationalization of a personal spirit who experiences life superficially.

Casual or recreational sex is a sellout to a lower self. Such a self has not caught the vision of how wonderful a sexual relationship can be when it is blessed by God and entered into with a sense of its true holiness. It is difficult for any of us to escape the way our culture seduces us to think of beauty. We get hung up on slender young bodies as the standard of sexuality. When a wife has carried several children and her body is not as "shapely" as it was before, a husband can easily be drawn to some new and "beautiful" young thing who wanders into his life. Without an awakened personal spirit to stimulate true conscience, he may act on his impulses and become sexually involved outside marriage. In doing this he throws away the glory. And the sad part is, he may not even realize that there was glory to throw away. Of course, women as well can react similarly toward their husbands, falling into the same traps.

Lord,

Break me out of the tyranny of my immediate problems and desires. Help me to remember past events responsibly and experience hope for tomorrow. Enable me to meet others, to communicate beyond words, to get in touch with my own feelings, and especially the feelings of others.

Teach me the holiness and glory of sexual intimacy with my spouse. Set me free from fear of vulnerability and the greed of self-gratification. Enable me to cherish and bless my mate with every cell of my being.

Forgive my past sexual sins by which I have wounded God, others, and myself. Separate my spirit from that of every other person with whom I have been intimate. Wash me clean, and enable me to relate wholly and only to my spouse. Amen.

CHAPTER 4 AWAKENING EXERCISES

1. Review the four characteristics of an awakened personal spirit listed in this chapter. Rate yourself on a scale of 1 to 5 (1= least awake, 5= most awake) by circling the degree to which you feel your spirit is in an awakened state for each.

   The ability to transcend time

1	2	3	4	5

   Communicating with others on a deep level

1	2	3	4	5

   Sustaining long-term personal relationships

1	2	3	4	5

   Experiencing the glory of Christian marital sex

1	2	3	4	5

2. Now, have your spouse or a close friend rate you using the same scale, without having seen your answers.

3. Write down, or discuss with your group, three lessons you have learned from past mistakes in dealing with others. Tell how these lessons have helped you avoid repeating mistakes in the present.

   _____

   _____

_____

_____

_____

4. In what areas of your life do you consider yourself to be most vulnerable to making decisions without fully considering the consequences? Discuss with your group or a friend how you could improve on making more careful and sensible life decisions.

5. Describe your feelings about sharing your very personal concerns with others. Is it irritatingly uncomfortable to be self-revealing and vulnerable, or do you find it refreshing? Do you have several friends with whom you regularly share from your heart? If so, what might it take to free you up to be more intimate in your communication with them?

_____

_____

_____

_____

6. Is your spirit awake enough to regret having lost touch with a number of people you formerly considered to be close friends? Why did you lose touch? Do you see the need to rebuild those relationships? Write down

the names of three people you will call or write this
week to get back in touch! Share this commitment with
your group or a friend to encourage you and hold you
accountable to follow through.

_____

_____

_____

_____

7. How do you feel about the role of sex in your life? Is sex
    for you a glorious and holy experience? What actions
    or attitudinal changes are you willing to take to help
    restore your sex life to a high plane of spirituality?
    Discuss the relationship of sex and your spiritual aware-
    ness with your spouse or the one you love. Consider
    whether this is an issue important enough to deal with
    together in Christian counseling or prayer ministry.

_____

_____

_____

_____

_____

8. If you have, in the past, thrown away the glory and
    uniqueness of marital sex by having union with others,
    before or during marriage, go to someone whose confi-
    dentiality you can trust (preferably a pastor or priest)
    and make confession (James 5:16). Ask for absolution
    (pronouncement of forgiveness) as in John 20:23. Ask
    for prayer that your spirit will be loosed from every
    person with whom you have had illicit union, that you
    will be made free and holy to your spouse (Matthew
    16:19; 18:18).

    _____

    _____

    _____

    _____

    _____

5

RELATING TO SELF

D O YOU CHARACTERISTICALLY MAINTAIN A healthful and positive attitude and rebound from minor illnesses with quick resilience? Physical health is definitely related to the condition of the personal spirit. We cannot separate body and mind, body and soul, or body and spirit. Our spirit is the life force within us. Scripture speaks of this in a very concrete way in Proverbs 18:14: "A man's spirit sustains him in sickness, but a crushed spirit who can bear?"

My son, pay attention to what I say;
listen closely to my words.

Do not let them out of your sight,
   keep them within your heart;
for they are life to those who find them
   and health to a man's whole body.
Above all else, guard your heart,
   for it is the wellspring of life.

—PROVERBS 4:20–23

Have you noticed how some people cave in to illness? When they become sick, it really gets them down. They feel their sickness deeply and they have little resilience to bounce back quickly to good health. Their illnesses seem to drag on and on.

On the other hand, there are people who seem to have indomitable spirits. They are seldom ill and maintain a cheerful and positive demeanor even when they are feeling bad. They always seem to focus on the positive and are a joy to be around.

A few years ago a friend of ours attended a medical conference and later shared with us the insights he had gained from some research reports presented there. Doctors had been researching why some people of the same age and with the same illness and similar life circumstances achieve quick recoveries, while others progress more slowly or do not get well at all. The result of the study indicated that the patients who achieve the quickest recovery are usually those who demonstrate a grateful attitude toward life.

The vibrancy of one's personal spirit is the power source of one's will to live a positive and healthful life.

That finding is not the least bit surprising. Remember that the personal spirit is the basic life force of our being. Each of us is made by God as a living creature whose body, mind, soul, and spirit are intended to be linked together in a wonderful synergy of life. When the spirit is thwarted in its development, the body's ability to maintain physical health is directly affected.

Disease is a human condition from which no one can escape. We all get sick at some time or another. And for reasons we do not understand, even the most saintly persons are often attacked by debilitating diseases that cause suffering and death. But it is a well-documented fact that the will to live and the determination to fight disease with a positive attitude often have dramatic influence on how resistant a person is to the ravages of illness.

The vibrancy of one's personal spirit is the power source of one's will to live a positive and healthful life. If a slumbering spirit can be awakened, the body's ability to be healed or to maintain good health will greatly increase.

It is for this very reason that hospitals specializing in rehabilitation of the sick and injured employ all kinds of stimulating activities to renew the spiritual vitality of the patient. Music, reading, crafts, games, group interaction, entertainment, outings, religious services, counseling—all play a part in nurturing the spirit. These activities promote the spiritual-physical interaction in which healing can happen.

Therapists even bring pets into the rehabilitation centers to play with patients. A cute and friendly dog can do wonders to reawaken feelings of being loved and accepted unconditionally. Cancer patients are often treated with massage therapy because the soothing touch of human hands can ease tension, renew the spirit, and stimulate both emotional and physical healing.

People who have awakened personal spirits are active, are alive, enjoy life, have fun, and interact with friends and family. Their very aliveness helps them to sustain good health. Evaluate yourself!

- How do you feel about your general health?
- Do you perceive yourself as uncommonly vulnerable to illness?
- Are you often depressed? Do you find it difficult to maintain a positive attitude?
- Do you rebound very slowly from fatigue, a cold, or the flu?

If you answer yes to the last three questions, a slumbering spirit may be draining you of physical vitality.

BEING GUIDED BY A TRUE WORKING CONSCIENCE

Does your personal sense of right and wrong work powerfully to alert you to moral and ethical danger areas and enable you to make good decisions to stay out of trouble? Or does your conscience only become active afterward to remind you that you did wrong?

This characteristic of an awakened spirit is perhaps the most important one of all because the conscience is so essential to the way we function in the world—in our relationship to God and in our interactions with others.

There are two types of conscience—a *remorse conscience* and a *true conscience*. A remorse conscience will be of little help to keep you out of trouble because it only works after an event to remind you that you have done wrong. It is based in flesh (a bondage to the requirements of the law and the inner man's struggle with lawless desires). A remorse conscience expresses itself primarily as "I'm sorry. I failed." A person with a remorse conscience possesses very little awareness of the specifics of how his wrongful actions may affect others. He focuses primarily on how acceptable standards of behavior were violated. A remorse conscience does not produce true repentance and does not bring one's heart to Christ so that the old self can be put to death on the cross. Consequently, a remorse conscience never leads to inner healing.

A true conscience works on the basis of your personal spirit. It works before an event to prevent you from getting into trouble. It sings out, "Warning! Warning! Warning!" to alert you to the danger of temptation and the possible hurt that your wrongful actions might cause. A true conscience also can show you after an event what you have done to another person. It can cause you to hurt empathetically for the other person's sake, not just because you have failed to uphold the law of God.

Consider for a moment how a true conscience might work. You are in a meeting with a large group of people, and you see a lady who has a very nice purse. She is well dressed and would likely have quite a bit of money with her in the purse. Now suppose everyone leaves the room for a coffee break and she leaves her purse on the floor beside her chair. You are in the room by yourself. What's to keep you from stealing that purse?

The law says, "Thou shalt not steal." But the function of the law is not to keep us from sinning, is it? *The law is to convict us of sin, not to empower us not to sin.* Will fear stop you? Not likely! You're pretty courageous, and you are clever.

What does have the power to stop you from stealing the purse? The Lord lives in your spirit, and if your spirit is awake, the Lord gives you love for other people. Taking that woman's purse could wound her terribly. Therefore, because of your love for the Lord Jesus Christ and because of His love singing in your spirit for her, you can't allow yourself to steal.

Another element should be mentioned here as well. Jesus said that the second greatest commandment is to love our neighbor as we love ourselves. Implicit in that statement is that we should love ourselves. We should cherish our own integrity and our own high calling to Christian discipleship so that we cannot violate ourselves by choosing a course of action we know to be wrong.

> We know that we live in him and he in us, because he has given us of his Spirit.
>
> —1 JOHN 4:13

Our conscience helps us choose what is right because the love of God sings in us. We cannot do that which is wrong because it would wound Jesus Christ and it would wound the other person. It is not for self-centered reasons that a true and working conscience will not let us sin. It is because the love of the Lord impels the conscience to think of others. It is a social conscience, born of an awakened personal spirit.

People whose spirits slumber have a lessened capacity to think of how other persons will feel or how the consequences of an act might wound others. A slumbering spirit will keep a person from developing a true and working conscience even when we would least expect it, such as among Christian leaders.

This helps us to understand what happened with those evangelists and pastors mentioned previously who developed patterns of having sex with different women as they traveled from city to city. The Holy Spirit comes on a person, and as the Scripture says, "A man's gift maketh room for him" (Prov. 18:16, KJV). He is out there preaching and teaching or evangelizing, but he has never dealt with, within the depths of his heart, the reality of his own slumbering spirit. The Holy Spirit has come on him and works primarily through his mind. He also works through his hands. He can preach and teach brilliantly, and he can lay on hands for healing, but his own spirit is asleep. His conscience is not awake enough to block him from acting on his selfish and lustful desires.

This raises a question people have asked many times: "I thought that the very purpose of the Holy Spirit was to quicken our spirits and to bring us to life. So why aren't people like this awake if they have the Holy Spirit?"

We went to the Lord in prayer with this question, and He answered us in this way. A man can have a hardened heart that affects his personal spirit. Picture the Holy Spirit flowing over a man. It flows over his mind, and he preaches a beautiful sermon. It flows over his body, and he can lay on hands to heal the sick. It flows into his emotions, and he can stir the hearts of people. But picture his spirit like a boulder in the middle of a stream. The water flows around the boulder, but it is unmoved. The water surrounds it and rushes over it, but it cannot penetrate the stone. Some people are like that. The Holy Spirit is all around them and even working through them, but they are personally unaffected in their own personal spirit. Thus, they are vulnerable to falling into heinous sins.

In this context, take another look at what Jesus had to say:

> Many will say to me on that day, "Lord, Lord, did we
> not prophesy in your name, and in your name drive out
> demons and perform many miracles?" Then I will tell

them plainly, "I never knew you. Away from me, you evildoers!"

—Matthew 7:22–23

Lord,

I realize that the condition of my mind, my heart, and especially my spirit profoundly affects the health of my body.

Search my innermost being and help me to know my sin. I ask for the gift of deep repentance. Breathe a new and right spirit within me, Lord, and let my body reflect restored health from the inside out.

Let my conscience go to work as a shield against temptation, whether I am tempted to sin against myself or against others.

Waken my spirit so I can identify with the pain my actions will afflict on God, upon others, and upon the entire body of mankind. Amen.

CHAPTER 5 AWAKENING EXERCISES

1. Review the two characteristics of an awakened personal spirit listed in this chapter. Rate yourself on a scale of 1 to 5 (1 = least awake, 5 = most awake) by circling the degree to which you feel your spirit is in an awakened state.

    Maintenance of good health

    1   2   3   4   5

    Being guided by a true and working conscience

    1   2   3   4   5

2. Now, have your spouse or a close friend rate you on the same scale without seeing your answers. How do your ratings compare?

    _____

    _____

    _____

3. How do you actually feel about your general health? What is the response of your heart (not just your head) when someone asks, "How are you doing today?" and you respond mechanically by saying, "Fine"? How do you suppose your true feelings may reflect on the condition of your personal spirit?

_____

_____

_____

_____

4. Review the two kinds of conscience described in this chapter. Which seems most characteristic of you? What actions could you take to be more sensitive to developing a true and working conscience?

_____

_____

_____

_____

5. Has the experience of rating your level of an awakened spirit been painful, enlightening, or both? What areas of spiritual slumber concern you most?

_____

_____

_____

_____

6. Share your ratings and your feelings with a Christian friend or with your group members. What patterns do you detect in your self-evaluation that reveal where you need the most renurturing?

_____

_____

_____

_____

7. Talk with group members or a friend about how to help you achieve a more awakened personal spirit. Make a list of suggestions below.

_____

_____

_____

_____

8. Pray with friends or group members about your list. Have them pray aloud with you for your spirit to be awakened.

PART III

SPIRITUAL THERAPY—
WAKING THE SPIRIT

6

NURTURING YOUR CHILD'S SPIRITUAL VITALITY

S PIRITUAL NURTURE IS OUR WAY OF BRINGING YOUNG lives into a conscious awareness of a loving God. It is a step-by-step, day-by-day celebration of how we are connected to each other, to the world around us, and to God, who is the Creator and Sustainer of all life.

As nurturing parents, family, and friends, we do not create the personal spirit in children. We only provide the loving, fertile environment in which a child's personal spirit can unfold naturally. The personal spirit is the inner being that holds the breath of life within each of us. The Hebrew word *ruach* and the Greek word *pneuma* are the words used for this breath or wind from God that flows through us to give us life. To be an agent of healthy nurture is to stay attuned to the natural wonder of a child's discovery and enthusiasm for all of life—to encourage emotional sensitivity and expression, not to discourage and stifle it.

> The quality of our nurture is the single most important element affecting the future spiritual and mental health and wholeness of our children.

It is difficult to stay focused on the wonder and responsibility of spiritual nurture when so much of our daily life is measured in seemingly ordinary moments. This is particularly true amid the stress of nightly awakenings, diaper changes, dirty dishes, and endless hours of rocking a colicky baby. But what we do with and for our children, particularly from the time of birth until the age of six, will have a lasting impact on the rest of their lives.

The following are six key ways of spiritual nurturing:

1. Building trust by much affectionate touch
2. Establishing loving discipline
3. Staying open to the wonder of discovery
4. Building a supportive family life
5. Teaching and modeling attitudes and behavior

6. Talking on our children's level so they can understand us, and listening to their hearts as well

BUILDING TRUST

A baby learns trust by feeling secure. This comes through being gently and carefully held, touched, snuggled, loved, and played with. Infants need this physical contact to begin to develop connectedness with other people beyond themselves and their mother. Ideally, this affectionate cuddling should come both from parents and other family members. But the father, as mentioned previously, has a special responsibility as he assumes his God-given role as parent and co-nurturer.

Some fathers, whether out of fear of not knowing what to do or out of misplaced role modeling, admire their children from a distance, but they leave the physical care of the baby to the mother. Fathers should be aware that babies need their attention and loving touch. A baby needs the father's presence and attentive nurture to build the simple trust and first feelings of corporateness essential to an awakened personal spirit.

On the other hand, some fathers, in the exuberance of young parenthood, are tempted to become a little too active in their attempts to play with their newborn baby. Wild swinging to and fro, throwing the baby into the air and catching him, or dropping the baby suddenly and catching him in mid-fall are healthy and needed. But if these actions are too severe or are done before baby is ready, they are not likely to build the kind of security and trust an infant needs to develop. And they can possibly lead to physical injury.

Gentle rocking while being securely held and other nonthreatening stimulation are first needed. As the child grows and becomes more responsive and playful, he will naturally let you know when he is ready for more adventurous fun.

As a baby moves from infancy into childhood, trust takes on a broader meaning. Touching is still important, and playtime is a natural expression of that physical intimacy. But children also need to feel secure in their parents' love as it is expressed in other ways. Being present, being attentive, being consistent, and being unselfishly fair are the basic ingredients that build trust in a child.

- A child who loses a grandparent or even a pet to death may need a lot of reassurance that you are not going to desert him in some way.

- A child whose parents separate or divorce needs a lot of special attention to overcome the insecurity of loss and to understand that his parents' problems are not his fault. If more parents understood the negative impact divorce can have on their children, perhaps they would work harder to salvage their marriage relationship for the sake of their children's welfare.

- ❧ A child who has two very busy working parents needs special times of focused attention with them to overcome the feeling of being an unimportant person in a busy world. A child needs to be able to trust in the knowledge that he is supremely important to the people who love him.

- ❧ A child needs to be able to trust his parents to be consistently believable. He needs promises to be kept and discipline to be administered consistently. He needs to observe his parents practicing what they preach.

ESTABLISHING LOVING DISCIPLINE

Discipline is an essential element in child rearing, but there is a distinct line between appropriately administered punishment to correct dangerous or inappropriate behavior and repeated intimidation and violent spankings that are abusive.

Common sense should tell us that a newborn baby should not be treated in the same way you would treat an older child who has reached the age of accountability. A baby is not a reasoning person who makes willful decisions to disobey. A baby cries when he is hungry, uncomfortable, or in pain and needs to be lovingly tended to reduce his discomfort. Spanking, shaking, angry shouting, or other kinds of physical coercion in an attempt to discipline a baby for crying has absolutely no place in healthy nurturing. During this stage of development, a child is not willfully disobeying and has no ability to understand the reason for such action. He can respond only with more discomfort, confusion, and insecurity—and his personal spirit will be suppressed.

Unfortunately, many parents have grown up in homes in which spanking of young babies and severe whipping of children was a common practice. Unless they can be brought to a more enlightened understanding, such parenting techniques are passed from one generation to another even when they are wrong and emotionally destructive.

When a child is old enough to explore his world by climbing under, around, and over everything in sight, the concept of discipline begins to take on legitimacy. Developmentally, the child can begin to learn cause-and-effect relationships, and appropriate discipline can begin the teaching of limits. The meaning of the word *no* can be reinforced by physically restraining a child from reaching for a dangerous object or going where he is not allowed. Although language comprehension is at a rudimentary level, a light slap on the hands accompanied by a firm no will begin to make an impression and establish needed limits on a child's behavior.

A typical example of this was when our grandson Joel first discovered that he could crawl into the bathroom and play with that wonderful roll of toilet paper. His first delight was to grab one end and crawl down the hall with the paper trailing off the spindle in a stream behind him. We all laughed, of course, and thought, "How cute!" However, the cuteness turned to trouble when Joel learned to reel off great armloads and dump it into the toilet until the bowl would become clogged.

Mother Victoria's initial scoldings were an ineffective deterrent, so she began to slap his little hands each time he would begin tearing the toilet paper. Although he could only talk in one- or two-word phrases, he soon got the point—"throwing paper in the bowl makes Mommy angry and gets my hands slapped." Joel showed us in a vividly nonverbal way that he was learning the lesson. One day after watching him crawl down the hall toward the bathroom, Victoria went to see what he was doing. Joel had cleverly closed the bathroom door. Inside she found him standing beside the stool, pulling at the toilet paper roll. When he turned around to see her watching, he held out one of his little hands and slapped himself just as his mother had done! Joel had learned his limits.

As a child grows older and his mind is more capable of weighing right against wrong and its consequences, discipline in its various forms can take on additional significance. Privileges, such as having special treats, watching TV, or playtime with friends, can be a reward for good behavior and can be withheld as a consequence of disobedience. Since spanking is the most severe form of punishment, it should only be reserved for the most severe transgressions, such as lying, stealing, and deliberate in-your-face defiance. Children need to learn in simple ways that they must bear responsibility for their actions and that decisions to disobey will result in predictable consequences.

I (Paula) remember being disciplined in many creative ways by my mother. I remember most clearly the times I misbehaved and my mother would send me to the backyard to cut a switch off the tree with which I would be whacked several times. Yes, the spankings always hurt enough to get my attention, but it was the trip to the backyard and the cutting of my own switch that I find indelibly printed in my mind.

In retrospect, I think my being sent to cut my own switch served two distinct purposes. That trip to the backyard to cut my own switch always gave me time to pause and ponder what I had done and the consequences I was to suffer. The trip reinforced in my mind what my mother's expectations were. It also gave my mother time to cool down and not spank me in anger. I would always get the spanking, but it was from a more collected mom who could calmly explain just why I was being disciplined and who would express her love and support for me following the punishment.

The Scriptures speak of the need for discipline and even of the appropriateness of a spanking when needed.

> He who spares the rod hates his son, but he who loves him is careful to discipline him.
>
> —PROVERBS 13:24

> Fathers, do not provoke your children to anger; but bring them up in the discipline and instruction of the Lord.
>
> —EPHESIANS 6:4, NAS

Do not withhold discipline from a child; if you punish
him with the rod, he will not die. Punish him with the
rod and save his soul from death.

—PROVERBS 23:13–14

Discipline, and especially a spanking, should always be
followed with expressions of love. Think of it this way. If
discipline is administered to you without love, it means that
your soul is being hauled to account, your mind is hauled to
account, and your emotions are pulled up short. Discipline
by itself may bring you under control, but your spirit is likely
to retreat and sit sullenly in a hole. You may come back into
the family to participate, but not all of yourself will be there.
Your spirit will stay in retreat or be provoked to resentment
and anger.

If discipline is followed by expressions of love and hugs,
then your spirit is drawn out again to be part of the family and
to want to be there. This teaches the child that discipline and
love go together. A child needs to understand that discipline is
for his own good and it costs the parent pain to do it. Children
need to experience loving touch right after discipline.

There are several things about loving discipline that should
be remembered.

Never cause more pain than the crime deserves.

Discipline may include an occasional spanking to establish
consequences for inappropriate behaviors. But severe spankings or any other kind of physical violence that inflicts bruises,

cuts, or other tissue damage to a child is clearly abusive and ceases to produce the character formation desired.

Similarly, a child can benefit from a verbal reprimand, but constant verbal attack and its subsequent emotional trauma are also abusive and counterproductive to a child's healthy nurture. When a child is continually called stupid or told he is a bad person, his self-concept will suffer. He will begin to believe it, and his spirit will be stifled.

For toddlers who have a well-developed understanding of language and are able to remember their transgressions, the loss of a privilege may be a more effective way to discipline. For instance, our two-year-old granddaughter Briana loved to watch Walt Disney movies. If she resisted going to bed at night, persistent disobedience was usually stopped when she was firmly told, "If you get out of your bed one more time, you will not be allowed to watch your movie tomorrow."

Effective discipline requires consistency, firmness, and love.

Consistency of discipline is important so as not to confuse a child. If a reprimand or spanking is given for an offense on one occasion and then overlooked the next time, the lesson will hold little value for a child. Parents should make their expectations very clear; otherwise the child will have no sense of what the boundaries are.

Loving discipline achieves its effects without fear.

Loving discipline preserves the integrity of the spirit and allows a child to learn the lesson and bounce back without the lingering impact of fear. Abuse produces fear, but discipline allows us to grow strong. This is an important lesson in building strong character in children. Through loving discipline, they learn to take rebuke and yet retain the security that they will continue to be loved. Later in life, when setbacks befall them, they will have the strength of character to accept the responsibility for their wrongs, take whatever comes, and know that they can handle life's setbacks.

> Our fathers disciplined us for a little while as they thought best; but God disciplines us for our good, that we may share in his holiness.
>
> —Hebrews 12:10

Staying Open to the Wonder of Discovery

As we become more open to the life-giving energy that flows naturally from children, we cannot help but be transformed ourselves. We grow alongside our children, and if we allow ourselves, we learn to freely play again and discover a rebirth of joy and delight that may have fallen asleep within us years ago. For adults preoccupied with an adult world and the pressures of career and home, this can be a difficult transition.

My (Lee) wife, Carol, tells of a dream she had during the late stages of pregnancy with our son, Matthew. She was an account executive for a major insurance company and traveled frequently, dealing professionally with executives in government agencies. In her dream she saw herself in the hospital giving birth to our son. When the nurses brought the baby to her for the first time, they sat him down on her chest. He was dressed in a three-piece business suit, carried a junior-sized briefcase, and began a conversation with her.

Absurd? Perhaps. But her subconscious mind threw up a role-conflict image that is common to many parents. Fortunately, in real life, her new role of nurturing mother came very easily. The ensuing months of quiet time, snuggling, and playing with and nurturing her baby became the happiest and most richly rewarding times of her life.

The point is that babies and very young children aren't just junior adults and cannot be treated as such. They need the time and attention of parents who will get down on the floor and play with them on their developmental level, lovingly and gently helping them to explore their new environment and to keep open the wonder of new life unfolding. Parents should always be available for hand holding, hugging, and snuggling with a child to communicate the security of connectedness that is nurtured through touch.

Helping children stay open to the wonder of discovery doesn't have to be a chore. It mostly means paying attention to what interests and excites them at each developmental stage of their lives and trying not to stifle that natural curiosity and sense of good fun.

Instead of saying no, lest children get themselves dirty or interrupt you as you hurry to get to the next place you are rushing to, take the time to let them splash in the puddle, look at the bug, or watch the sparrows sitting on the telephone line.

If you want to organize their wonder of discovery into more regimented activities to teach them to coordinate with others' schedules, try paying attention to how you can make an adventure out of such things as mealtime, bath time, bedtime, chore time, and playtime. Or try starting meaningful family rituals or traditions. Here are a few suggestions to get your mind churning.

Mealtime

Let your kids get involved in the meal by helping to peel the potatoes or carrots, stir the soup, sprinkle the seasoning, or set the table. Make a nest in their mashed potatoes for green pea eggs. Make their hot cakes in the shape of hearts or crescent moons. Let them make smiley faces with mustard on their sandwiches. Ask their advice on how to cook. Let it be a learning experience.

Kids love romance and the unusual. Occasionally try mealtime as a formal occasion. Let them make place cards for seating. Try eating by candlelight. Ring a bell for the "waiter" to pass you seconds. On other occasions, spread a blanket on the floor and make the meal a picnic.

Have an occasional "caveman meal" in which everyone eats with their fingers. Serve the food on plastic wrap with no utensils. Maybe it will help them appreciate the practicality of plates, forks, and good manners.

Bath time

Fun bath time is when your child can take whatever toys he or she wants to the tub and stay as long as desired. If your kids get fussy when the water gets cold, show them how to warm it up. If they balk at washing their hair, let them do it with swimming goggles on to keep the soap out of their eyes.

Bath time can also be made special by lighting candles and playing a CD of classical music. Or you can put in a favorite sing-along CD.

Bedtime

If you are always short of time and in a hurry to get your child to bed, try reading the bedtime story while he or she is in the bathtub. Record yourself reading a favorite bedtime story. Then let your child take the recording and book to bed alone and follow along in the book to your recorded voice.

Chore time

Try to make household chores fun. Suggest that your kids pretend that dirt is the bad guy. Let them use squirt guns to spray window cleaner and then capture the bad guy by wiping the surface dry with a paper towel.

Most kids love to polish. Let them shine up the silverware or dust and polish the dining table.

Give your kids a choice among several chores they would like to do—vacuum carpets, dust furniture, fold clothes, and so on. Work alongside them to instruct and to offer praise for jobs well done—and for the fun of fellowship.

Playtime

Go for a neighborhood nature walk. Let kids take paper bags and pick up anything from nature that they find interesting. Talk about the objects as they are found or afterward at home. Emphasize the beauty of God's creation. Start a collection. Be careful not to superimpose your value judgment on what objects hold wonder. Their interests may be quite different from yours and should be cherished, understood, and talked about.

Save old and unusual clothes, shoes, and hats for a dress-up box. Have a weekly dress-up and pretend time. Encourage your children and the neighbor children to dress up and create a play about their imaginary characters.

Get your child to write a letter to the author of a favorite storybook. Chances are good that you will get a nice reply.

Organize a field trip to take several children to an interesting place like a local bakery, fire station, factory, and the like.

Family rituals

Always hold hands in family unity to say grace before meals. (You might even try sitting down at the dining table for meals instead of eating in front of the TV.)

Make a daily "hug sandwich" with parents on the outside as the bread and kids in the middle as the peanut butter and jelly, all squeezing together.

Encourage children to help put a family photo album together, and add to it regularly. Tell them your family history. Show them photos of your ancestors so they can recognize and tell stories about them. This builds a sense of roots of personal history and belonging.

Establish a ritual of blessing your children each morning before they go off to school. Stop them at the door or in the car before they get out. Place your hands on them and pray something similar to this: "Dear God, we ask Your blessing today on this Your child. Help him to have a wonderful and happy learning experience at school. Help him to do his very best. Keep him safe from harm. We bless him now with our love in Jesus's name. Amen."

BUILDING A SUPPORTIVE FAMILY LIFE

If a child is to grow up with the ability to love, empathize, and relate to others in a responsible way, he must learn what it is to live in community with others. This begins with parents—first in intimacy with the mother, then in contact with the outside world, hopefully with a loving and nurturing father.

Beyond that, a child greatly benefits in being surrounded by an extended family of brothers and sisters, cousins, aunts and uncles, and close family friends. These important persons become extensions of the child's self. If a primary family exists to surround the child with this community of love, nurturing of the child should be encouraged by creating opportunities for the entire family to come together and share.

The reality of our world is that many children are born into single-parent homes or homes that have a limited or nonexistent natural support system of grandparents or other blood relatives who live nearby. If this is the case, a nurturing parent should look for every opportunity to develop a network of loving friends who can become an important support group for a growing child.

Increasing numbers of aware Christians are responding to this need. The church is still the best place for parents to find the quality of nurture children require. Look for caring, loving friends to become your "family" through Sunday school classes and Bible study groups, and also in home prayer groups.

 Be a friend and make friends. Share of yourself and let others into your life. Ask for their commitment to help you and your child grow. This is what the church should be.

At a very early age, a child who lives in a family context will begin to pick up what it means to belong. The family doing things together builds a sense of identity and belonging in the spirit of the child. From peekaboo to patty-cake, the happy interaction of child and siblings and adult relatives begins to nurture a powerful sense of community.

In her wonderfully insightful book titled *Something More, Nurturing Your Child's Spiritual Growth,* Jean Grasso Fitzpatrick refers to three strong functions of the family as a nurturing community.

1. The family is a living embodiment of what it means to be spiritual, to have a place in community, to value people more than things, and to be sustained by sacred bonds of relationships.

2. The family functions as a community of memory; children see their own lives in the context of family stories and events, and they begin to understand how they and their family relate to the broader context of society.

3. The home gives children a perspective on the wider world; it sets the example for relating in ministry or dealing with justice toward others in the extended human family.[1]

Children are very impressionable and often become nostalgic about what their families do at special times of celebration, whether it is an event such as a marriage, a holiday, or even a family reunion. "What was it like when you got married, Mom and Dad?" "Tell us how Grandpa used to cut down and decorate the Christmas tree." "What did your family do on Thanksgiving when you were a little girl, Aunt Barbara?"

Take care to make holidays special occasions when the family is together. And even more than that, celebrate the significance of holidays by talking about or acting out the reason for the event.

As children grow and begin to comprehend the meaning of special events, take time to discuss what we are thankful for on Thanksgiving, and spend family time together in prayer. Hang out the flag and visit a cemetery on Memorial Day, and make an object lesson of why we remember those who gave their lives to secure our freedom and our peace. With a nativity scene, act out the events surrounding Jesus's birth on Christmas Day. Explain how gift exchanges are our way of responding to the gift God gave the world by sending His Son. Make real the awful events and meaning of Good Friday and the wonderful Easter message of the raising of Jesus from the dead.

On every possible occasion, share as a family. Sit together at church and at meals. Eat, talk, play, and sing together. Family togetherness builds ability within the spirit to be open, to relate, and to function in corporateness.

TEACHING AND MODELING
ATTITUDES AND BEHAVIOR

I (John) can remember my mother's words ringing in my ears. "Jackie, a gentleman never curses in front of a lady, or any other time." "Jackie, a man never hits a woman. Any man who hits a woman is no man at all." "Jackie, a gentleman treats his wife with courtesy and respect at all times. He never insults her or hurts her. He treats her like a lady at all times."

That teaching might have found no lodging place in me had I not seen my father model it in his own life. Children learn what you model more than what you say. I never heard my father raise his voice to my mother or say an insulting or cross word to her. I heard him and saw him treat her with respect at all times. I saw affection from him to her continually. I saw him comfort her. Those lessons, modeled by my parents, have been written in my heart.

If you don't want your child to lie, cheat on tests at school, or steal from friends, begin by paying attention to how fairly you deal with business clients, how much integrity you show in abiding by the law, and how honest you are about taking advantage of other people or their property. If you don't want your children to drink or take drugs, pay attention to the example you are setting for them. It's not enough to say, "Some things are for adults, and when you are old enough, this will be OK." Very simply, practice what you preach, or don't be surprised when your children pick up on your worst habits. If you are concerned enough about setting the right example for your child that you are willing to change your questionable behavior, your changed behavior will reap positive benefits in your life as well.

Talking So Kids Will Listen

Effective communication is an essential ingredient in keeping the personal spirit alive in children as they grow older. Good communication skills are a learned behavior and require a concerted effort to remain open and effective.

Adele Faber and Elaine Mazlish have written a wonderfully helpful guidebook, *How to Talk So Kids Will Listen and Listen So Kids Will Talk,*[2] for parents. The principles taught in this book are not particularly new, although the book has enlightened thousands of parenting study groups and has revolutionized communication within thousands of families. What Faber and Mazlish teach are commonsense approaches to helping parent-child communication stay open and constructive rather than closed and repressive.

All of us as parents should consider carefully how we relate to our children in daily conversation. Does our conversation impart the positive support and nurture they need to stay vibrantly alive in their spirits? Or does our constant critical and judgmental attitude cause them to retreat into woundedness?

The following overview of ways to more openly communicate with children should be helpful to avoid falling into the trap of judgment and criticism:

- Pay attention to what your children have to say. Take the time to listen quietly and attentively.

- Acknowledge the reality of your children's feelings. Even though you may have to modify the mode of delivery, do not try to deny a child the honest expression of that emotion.

- Help children identify feelings by giving the feelings a name or description; for example, "What I hear is that you get very angry when you are treated that way," or perhaps, "Getting a good grade on your test today certainly has put you in a happy mood this afternoon."

- When you discover a problem, avoid heavy or repetitive scolding. Rather, simply describe what you see so you can call it to their attention; for example, "I see you chose not to clean your room this morning. I hope you understand it must be done before you go out this afternoon."

- Give enough information so that it can be understood why an action is a problem; for example, "I don't want you to come into the kitchen on roller skates because the rollers will damage the tile floor."

⋈ Be brief and to the point in communicating your desire, even as brief as one word, to call attention to a problem that has been discussed previously; for example, when the child appears at the kitchen door with roller skates on, simply say, "The skates!" (But say it lightly; they will pick up on every ounce of irritation or condemnation.)

⋈ Clearly communicate to your children the expectations of what you consider to be acceptable and unacceptable behavior. They need to know what the boundaries are.

⋈ Describe how you feel to your children— what you like and what you don't like; for example, "I like it when you remember to tell me where you are going and when you will return," or perhaps, "It makes me angry to think that you deliberately disobeyed my instructions."

⋈ Give children a choice between options to avoid rigid confrontations and to help them develop autonomy; for example, "Which do you prefer? Stay home and go to the party or go on the camping trip?" Or, "Which outfit will you wear, your coat with a tie or a white shirt and sweater?"

≫   Show respect for the ways children struggle to solve problems, make decisions, or learn by experience; for example, "I know it must have been hard for you not to argue with your teacher when you felt falsely accused, but you showed maturity in making that decision."

≫   Encourage children with helpful advice rather than taking over and doing things for them; for example, "When you fry bacon, try turning the fire down lower so it will cook more slowly. Then it will be less likely to burn."

≫   Don't probe for information or ask too many questions. Encourage discussion with open-ended statements like, "Tell me about your day." With younger children, be more specific to help them find descriptive words.

≫   Don't rush to answer children's questions as though you are always the authority. Rather, ask them what they think to help sharpen their problem-solving skills and turn the question into a two-way discussion.

❧ Encourage children to include sources outside the home for information. Help them experience research to discover needed information; for example, "Why don't we stop at the pet store so you can ask them what they think is the best way to house-break a new puppy?"

❧ Don't take away hope by discouraging new experiences or activities that might stretch a child's ability; for example, "It may be tough to make the team because you are younger than the other boys, but trying out will be good experience whether you make it or not."

❧ Call attention to the positive things you observe. Give praise when it is deserved; for example, "I saw how you responded positively to the coach's criticism of your play today. You were careful to do it right the next time. You're becoming a good athlete because you are coachable."

❧ Describe what you see when you observe positive behavior; for example, "I see you did all your chores this morning. Now you'll have the rest of the day to do whatever you like."

⊰ Describe how you feel when you are pleased
or proud; for example, "I was so proud of you
today, the way you set a good example for
the younger children."

⊰ Model the behavior you would like to see
in your child; for example, "I cleaned out
the garage today and have several things to
donate to The Salvation Army thrift store.
Would you like to donate some of the toys
you don't play with anymore so some other
children might enjoy them?"[3]

The basic elements essential to the development of a
healthy and awakened personal spirit are really very simple.
Despite the pressures that are a normal part of any household, children need affectionate touching, the loving presence of a family, focused time with good communication,
guided exploration, gentle discipline, and love.

> *Lord,*
>
> *Write it on my heart that I will never in all
> my life have opportunity to influence a life as
> profoundly as I will with the children You have
> placed under my care.*
>
> *Equip me with a listening ear; an under-
> standing and loving heart; arms that embrace
> with clean, wholesome affection; and a tongue
> that praises and encourages.*

Give me Your wisdom to discipline consistently and appropriately with unconditional love.

Make me an attractive model for joyful adventure in discovering the wonders of Your creation. Amen.

Chapter 6 Awakening Exercises

Significant strides can be made in effective nurturing of children if husbands and wives will stay focused, be consistent in promoting a balanced and stimulating lifestyle, and regularly talk about how to work at it together.

Review the six suggested nurturing areas in this chapter. Then duplicate the outline below to structure one focused activity in each area that you can schedule and practice during each week. Use this list as a daily reminder of ways to improve your ability to nurture a child's developing personal spirit.

Begin keeping a daily journal of thoughts, feelings, activities, successes, failures, and memorable experiences you have with your child. Let your journal help you grow daily in spiritual vitality along with your child.

Weekly "Child-Nurturing" Activities and Awarenesses

1. Ways I can build trust:

    _____

    _____

    _____

    _____

2. Ways I can establish loving discipline:

_____

_____

_____

3. Ways I can help my children stay open to the wonder of discovery:

_____

_____

_____

4. Ways I can help to build a supportive family life:

_____

_____

_____

5. Ways in which I can discipline myself to teach and model behavior better than I have:

_____

_____

_____

6. Ways I can improve family communication by talking so kids will listen, and listening so kids will talk:

_____

_____

_____

7

RISE AND SHINE: REAWAKENING YOUR SPIRIT

O NE CANNOT EXPECT TO AWAKEN THE PERSONAL spirit simply by being aware that the problem exists. This is perhaps a misconception born out of the way some psychoanalytical counseling is practiced— that if one becomes adequately aware of a problem, the self-awareness will naturally result in a solution and healing. You cannot change what you do not recognize and acknowledge. However, you must want to change, and you must be willing to seek and accept the process of loving nurture that can awaken your spirit.

Your spirit slumbers because you have closed your heart in reaction to a wounding, and this has anesthetized your precious life energy. To awaken your spirit, you must go through a process of both healing and renurturing. The healing process entails working through forgiveness toward those who either wounded you and/or neglected to give the nurture your spirit required. It will not suffice merely to apply the many practical suggestions listed elsewhere in this book. Listening to uplifting music, reading good books, playing with friends, and so forth are all good and needful exercises to awaken the spirit, but these will not complete the task without inner healing.

HEALING YOUR SLUMBERING SPIRIT

Healing your slumbering spirit is accomplished first through open and honest sharing of life's experiences with a friend, a small group, a pastor, or even better—a prayer minister. That time ought not to be foreshortened. The sharing itself is cathartic and healing, for one of the main reasons your spirit fell asleep in the first place was that you shut off your feelings long ago. The friend or prayer minister needs to know as much as time allows about the person's life. Through sharing, the Holy Spirit is given opportunity to reveal secrets of the heart; "everything that becomes visible is light" (Eph. 5:13, NAS). Knowledge informs prayer.

The helper(s) and the one being healed can pray about whatever bitter roots are discerned. A beneficial root is a practiced, hidden way of drinking nurture from God, others, ourselves, and nature. Roots are "practiced and hidden" because our spirit learns to open and drink from others in earliest infancy, building automatic ways of opening to the presence and embrace of others in later life. At first, this involves choices (whether conscious or unconscious) to open and embrace. But after the habit is established, it becomes automatic and we forget that we ever learned how to meet others heart to heart—we just do it.

 Healing and renurturing are both needed to awaken the slumbering spirit.

But if we do not receive holding, cuddling, laughter, and loving touches, our spirit is tempted to recoil in hurt. We then choose (again, whether consciously or unconsciously) to build the opposite into our hearts—bitter roots. Hebrews 12:15 says, "See to it that no one comes short of the grace of God; that no root of bitterness springing up causes trouble, and by it many be defiled" (NAS). In contrast to a good root, a bitter root is a practiced, hidden way of drinking harm from God, others, ourselves, and nature. It is learned and built into us opposite the way good roots are, in reaction to the absence of holding, cuddling, laughter, and loving touches.

One might ask, "How can one drink harm from God?" Of course, God harms no one; it is our false picture of God from which we drink harm. As parents, all of us have seen our children misunderstand our well-intentioned approaches and interpret us as intending harm. The woeful fact is that rancorous families, in which there is anger and shouting and/or little wholesome affection, offer their children more than the usual temptation to view God as being either punitive or unloving.

Bitter roots operate by God's laws. All His laws were meant to add blessing to blessing. But when sin is committed, the same laws meant to bring life bring forth harm. Deuteronomy 5:16 is not only the one command among the ten that promises blessing if it is obeyed; it is also a dynamic description of the way life operates: "Honor your father and mother..." *that life may go well with you.* The rule is that in any way you honored your father and mother (especially in childhood), in that very area life will go well with you—unless something negative interferes. The inverse presents the issue that prayer ministers need to address: in whatever way you did not honor your father and mother, life will not go well with you—unless grace intervenes.

That law is compounded by a second: "Do not judge lest you be judged. For in the way you judge, you will be judged; and by your standard of measure, it will be measured to you" (Matt. 7:1–2, NAS). How can little children, raised in dysfunctional families, not dishonor their eminently dishonorable parents? How can they not judge and thus set in motion the law that they will themselves be judged? Life will not go well with them because they have dishonored. God understands, with grieving compassion, and does not blame them, but law is law. Unless He is given opportunity to apply His grace, troubled lives will manifest the absoluteness of His laws.

One of the most common effects of this is that we become more and more like those we judge. Roman 2:1 states, "Therefore you are without excuse, every man of you who passes judgment, for in that you judge another, you condemn yourself; for you who judge practice the same things" (NAS). Every one of us is a lawbreaker. We have all hated, and therefore have broken the commandment against murder (1 John 3:15). We have all looked lustfully upon someone, and thus have broken the commandment against adultery (Matt. 5:28). Therefore, if we judge others, we reap evil, and here is how: Matthew 6:14 says, "But if you do not forgive men, then your Father will not forgive your transgressions" (NAS). Our judgment causes the sin we share in common with the one we judged to remain in us. Hosea 8:7 indicates that this situation cannot remain static: "They sow the wind and reap the whirlwind." So not only does the sin remain in us, but it also grows. We become more and more like those we judge.

Suppose a child judges his parents for never holding him, singing to him, reading books to him, or doing all those special things parents do to bring children's spirits to life. That judgment will harden his heart. A hardened heart is less and less able to receive the very things it once craved. Therefore, if he does not forgive and repent for bitterness, by the time he is grown, he is likely to be just as incapable of giving nurture as his parents were before him. He will have become just as much a slumberer as they were, if not more so.

These immutable laws are compounded by another: "Do not be deceived, God is not mocked; for whatever a man sows, this he will also reap" (Gal. 6:7, NAS). When children dishonor their parents by judging them, if that judgment does not find its way to the cross, the judgment must be reaped. Harm is often reaped through loved ones and friends who become tempted to fulfill our bitter-root expectations. I judged my mother for having a cutting, critical tongue. Life would not go well for me in that area, for by law my judgment had to be meted back to me. Therefore, I tempted my wife, Paula, to be more critical than she would have been. Fortunately, I was aware of the need to take my judgment to the cross. For if I had not, I might easily have continued the process of closing my heart, a practice I began in childhood, and my spirit might have fallen asleep.

A boy's father often upbraided his son instead of affirming him. The son dishonored his father by judging him, a response that set in motion the law that his life would not go well. In adulthood, his judgments were meted back to him through work. His boss would come to him intending to compliment him and would be astounded at himself because he would instead rip at him. Unaware of the principles we teach, the man did not take his judgment to the cross in prayer and instead closed his spirit, which continued to become ever more slumbering. And so life goes, in one area of trouble or trauma after another. (We suggest studying our book *Transforming the Inner Man* to learn how to see and heal root causes.)

When bitter roots cause the heart to harden, the heart becomes less resilient in the face of pain, for bitterness closes it off to the grace of Christ that would otherwise strengthen it. "If my father and mother forsake me, the LORD will receive me" (Ps. 27:10). This increases the pain, making it more and more tempting to use inner vows to dull the pain. For instance, a child who is bitter because his father never notices the pictures he has drawn at school might vow that he doesn't need such attention. That inner vow becomes a stronghold (2 Cor. 10:4–5) that shuts out love and life. If he does not take it to the cross, then, as an adult, he may be unable to be attentive to his wife; one cannot give what he has shut out of his own heart. We have found that, invariably, slumbering spirits have made a series of inner vows (consciously or unconsciously) to keep out the pain: "I won't share what's inside." "I won't need hugs." "I won't need praise." "I won't ever cry." "I will be strong." "I will only rely on myself." As long as these vows are in place, they will effectively block out much of the work we do to awaken the spirit.

Therefore, when reactions to lack of parental nurture have caused the spirit to slumber, the remedy is not just praying for a person's spirit to be awakened and assigning helpful habits that feed the spirit and keep it alive. The personal spirit is afflicted by bitter reactions to early wounds and present reaping. If these are not seen and overcome by prayer, any attempts to awaken the spirit might be like pouring water into a bucket with holes.

What is needed? Confession of bitterness. Adults may be unaware of childhood resentments. It is helpful, but not imperative, that slumberers remember exact instances of such resentments and share them with those who would pray for their healing. Many chose to forget long ago in order to keep from feeling pain. But we can see that any child in dysfunctional circumstances would naturally be resentful and can just admit by faith, "Where there is a fruit there is a root. The fruit of my life indicates that I must have been resentful. Lord, please forgive me for using forget-fulness and suppression, not the cross, to 'heal' my heart. Come and truly heal my heart." Prayer ministers can help people reckon as dead on the cross whatever bitter-root judgments have been discerned. They can set people free from surfacing patterns of trauma that rewound and sicken the personal spirit. Friends can pray blessings in place of patterns of reaped troubles.

But it should be remembered that just as the practical suggestions listed elsewhere in this book (listening to uplifting music, reading good books, playing with friends, etc.) are not sufficient, inner healing alone will also not awaken the spirit. Neglect and the bitter roots and inner vows that are formed in reaction to it have the effect of putting the spirit into what might be likened to a deep freeze. Have you ever come in from a snowy day so cold to the bone that you could not feel the warmth of your cozy kitchen? The temperature there might have been a snug 72 degrees, but for five or ten minutes, it might have well been 20 degrees below zero! But you stuck with it, and finally you were able to warm up. In the same way, inner healing will bring your spirit in out of the "cold" of a hardened heart. But if you do not apply the insights listed in the rest of this book, you might as well have brought your spirit into a kitchen where the heat has not been turned on. Both inner healing and these other suggestions are equally needed.

If adult sinning has caused the spirit to fall asleep and become incapable of functioning, once again, praying for awakening and then practicing habits that feed the spirit will not always suffice. There needs to be fulsome repentance and turning from evil. Prayers that pronounce forgiveness must be administered. But then the questions will still need to be addressed: "Was there an earlier wounding that left the person vulnerable to temptation?" "If so, what bitter reactions to harmful events, usually in childhood, created character flaws that could enable demonic forces to tempt you toward sinful choices?" These need to be investigated and brought to God's light and healing.

Those who wish to come alive again after sin has darkened their personal spirits need to humble themselves before friends who can be counted on to keep confidentiality, or visit with accomplished prayer ministers until the root causes of sinful behavior are discovered, placed under the blood, and put to death on the cross. Continuing guilt sickens the personal spirit, but the Lord's grace heals and sets free.

If a slumberer is slumbering because he or she has wandered away from prayer, worship, and fellowship, we should again ask if there are any root causes that need to ferreted out. What in the person's life and resultant character structures lies behind his defections? Why did the person wander away? Exploration should be extensive (perhaps with the input of those who know the person and can see him more clearly than he sees himself) and honestly entered into to allow the Holy Spirit access to uncover whatever lies hidden in the heart.

David said, "Deliver me from bloodguiltiness, O God, Thou God of my salvation; then my tongue will joyfully sing of Thou righteousness" (Ps. 51:14, NAS). Do you see the progression? "Deliver me...*then* my tongue will sing joyfully..." Revelation, confession, repentance, forgiveness, and healing are what successfully awaken personal spirits—and keep them joyfully alive and functioning.

Awakening slumbering spirits is a delight. Whoever assists celebrates being in partnership with God's Holy Spirit as He revives and heals. It is a joy to see people come alive. Healing slumbering spirits is a joyous work of resurrection. The father of the prodigal celebrated, "...this son of mine was dead, and has come to life again" (Luke 15:24, NAS). Those who minister to slumbering spirits resonate with the prodigal son's father. We don't have fatted calves to kill for the celebration, but we can join in praising God as slumberers see and feel what they have been blind and dead to.

We need only complete the resurrection by making sure to heal the root causes.

How to Awaken the Spirit

For an adult, renurturing one's personal spirit is a choosing process. It is not something someone else can choose for you. Nor is it something for which you can count on God for a quick miracle, something that will be "instantly fixed" by prayer. We should always remember that our journey in life, no matter how difficult and how fragmented, is a journey of daily decision making supported by a loving God of grace.

Many people have found that writing in a journal is a very helpful way to sort through the impact of situations and to make sense of jumbled feelings. There is something about the process of putting our experiences down in words that helps us gain clarity of understanding and be more ready to choose a positive direction in our daily journey.

I (Lee) often have found journaling both revealing and healing in my own struggle to achieve a more awakened personal spirit. During a time in which I was undergoing difficult life transitions and fighting debilitating depression, journaling helped me sort through the tangled underbrush of frustration and find a refreshing meadow of a cleared mind. Sometimes I wrote stream-of-consciousness prose, and sometimes I focused deeply and wrote poetry.

In the fifth and sixth chapters of his letter to the Ephesian church, the apostle Paul gave a wonderfully concise list of positive actions Christians should take to come into the fullness of life in Jesus Christ. We mentioned these earlier, but they bear repeating in paraphrased form. Follow these admonitions, and you will have taken the first series of steps on a journey toward wholeness of your personal spirit.

- ⇥ Be careful and choose wisely how you will live (Eph. 5:15).

- ⇥ Find out what pleases the Lord and be imitators of Christ (Eph. 5:17).

- ⇥ Stay away from intoxicants that will drug your senses and make you susceptible to immorality (Eph. 5:18).

- ⇥ Seek opportunities to relate to others lightheartedly, with laughter, singing, and Spirit-filled fun (Eph. 5:19).

- ⇥ Give thanks to God for everything life brings (Eph. 5:20).

- ⇥ Submit to each other in love and trust as Christian brothers and sisters (Eph. 5:21).

⤴ Be honorable in your family relationships by treating others with respect and consideration (Eph. 6:1–4).

⤴ Seek the Lord for strength, nurture, and cherishing. Be confident in His power to nurture and protect you (Eph. 6:10–12).

Reawakening your personal spirit cannot be accomplished by yourself. It is a process that requires help from others. Even if you are seeking help through a prayer minister, it is unlikely that the healing and nurture can happen adequately only in that one-on-one relationship. The awakening of the spirit happens best and most effectively through sharing relationships within a small group.

Persons who are slumbering in spirit need friends who will love them back to life. With this in mind, we give the following suggestions to seek an awakening of your personal spirit and to sustain your spirit as a vital life force.

1. Explore ways in which your spirit may be asleep.

Be aware of your shortcomings and the areas of your life in which you are experiencing difficulty. Take inventory of your feelings and behavior to evaluate what kinds of activities prompt the most excitement and aliveness in you and what activities generate little interest. How many of the following questions can you answer affirmatively?

- ⋇ When talking with others, do you understand and communicate with them on a feeling level without getting too thoughtful as to the right things to say?

- ⋇ Do you easily empathize with your friends by weeping with their sadness? Do you share their rejoicing without being overly intellectual?

- ⋇ Are you able to sustain close relationships with people over a long period of time?

- ⋇ Are you enjoying life and participating fully with others in activities that are fun?

- ⋇ Do you have a good sense of humor? Are you able to enjoy a good belly laugh?

- ⋇ Do you feel close to God and bask in His presence both in corporate worship and in private devotions without feeling that He is distant or that this is just a religious act of faith?

- ⋇ Do you feel spiritually alive?

- ⋇ Is sex with your spouse a holy meeting and not merely pleasurable sensations that might feel just as good with someone else?

- Does inspiration with new ideas and thoughts come quickly and easily for you?

- Do you thrill to good music and art?

- Does your conscience sing out forcibly, warning you of certain dangers you may encounter *before* you engage in a questionable behavior or event?

- Do you feel vibrantly alive and refreshed by being out in nature, or does this experience feel as flat as anything else?

Make a list of the areas of your life where you feel most asleep and where you would like to be rejuvenated. Thoughtfully review the nurturing relationships you have had with parents and significant others in your growing-up years. For the best effect, discuss these issues with a close friend or within a small group among those who understand.

- What were your parents like?

- How close did you feel to them while you were growing up?

- How physically expressive of love were your parents and other family members?

- In what ways did they support and encourage you?

- To what degree did they communicate vibrancy of life to you?

- What relationship do you have with your parents now?

- In what ways do you harbor ill will, anger, or regrets? (You may have more than you are aware of, but list those you recognize in yourself.)

- How willing are you to move beyond the past to forgive those who may have hurt you?

- How badly do you want to have a more fully awakened personal spirit?

2. Seek affection in your own family.

Seeking affection from parents or close relatives may be difficult if they have been part of the problem in the past, but a renewed effort to build more intimate relationships with family members is always in order. This can include talking that goes beyond the standard chitchat about TV shows, the weather, or the day's shopping expedition. Make an effort to share feelings and to speak from the heart in your conversations.

It may be frustrating to try to draw feelings out of others (particularly family members) who are not accustomed to sharing in this way. Do something special. Write a note, send a card, phone for no reason, and take the opportunity to pay someone a compliment. You cannot be responsible for their unwillingness to respond with affection, nor should you allow yourself to harbor anger for their inability. But you can be more open yourself and more willing to be vulnerable. You can practice asking others the kind of open and nonthreatening questions that will give them an opportunity to share.

Deepening your relationships also means paying attention to how you can express affection in more physical ways. Make a major effort to overcome any resistance you may have to giving and receiving hugs, holding hands, sitting close to others, or engaging in quiet, focused conversations that are uninterrupted by the TV, radio, or household duties. In small ways like this, the spirit can be refreshed and come to new levels of wakefulness.

Discuss with parents, brothers, sisters, aunts, uncles, and children the ways in which your family expresses or fails to express affection. If expressions of affection are lacking, encourage them to be more physically demonstrative. Ask for a hug. Embrace each other when greeting or parting. Hold hands to pray at special family gatherings or at mealtime. Try an occasional group hug, or sing a song together as a family as you stand in a circle with your arms around each other's shoulders. Begin to make those kinds of touching experiences a ritual of loving care. Some family members may not be able to do this. Their spirits may be too deeply asleep, but you will have tried.

3. Identify with Christian friends.

A wise prayer minister will recommend and arrange for the person to whom he or she is ministering to get involved in a small group to help with the healing and growth process. If this doesn't happen, start a group yourself. You don't have to make a big project of it. Ask among Christian friends with whom you have prayed or would like to pray. Invite them over for coffee or dinner. Ask if they would be interested in joining you to form a group to share, pray, love, and support one another. Then just begin.

If this seems to be difficult for you, remember the old adage that to have a friend you must be a friend. Building relationships requires presence, openness, and patience.

So often a person visits a church and almost expects to be rejected—with the attitude that the people there must meet certain standards to prove that they are friendly and accepting. Then when the church people don't take the "proper" initiative, the person can say that the church was an unfriendly group and he wouldn't have been happy there after all. Granted, the church is full of cliques, hypocrites, and sinners. But so is the world, only more so. The church still remains the most likely place to find people who will love you, accept you, and help you become your best self.

 If people have to guess your needs, it makes knowing you a task.

A little-known shortcut to getting what you want is to ask for it. If people have to guess your needs, it makes knowing you a task, and you are less likely to receive the kind of response that will help you heal your wounded spirit. Keep trying until you find that combination of friends who can really click together. Be patient but persistent. Not everyone is ready for the kind of sharing that can happen in the dynamics of a small group. But remember too that there are a lot of people in the world just like you who have the same kinds of life concerns and the same desires to grow in the Lord and to come alive in their spirits.

It often happens that a small group of close friends will help its members to become more awakened in their personal spirits just by getting together and expressing love to each other. Ideally, however, the group will be much more effective if its members are informed about inner healing and understand the concept of the slumbering spirit. So much more can be done if the group understands the specific kinds of requirements an individual in the group may have for coming alive.

The next chapter provides helpful guidelines on starting and conducting an effective small group.

4. Lighten your heart through good, clean fun.

Play as much as possible, and seek opportunities for enjoyment and recreation. Read uplifting books. Choose books of heroism, inspiration, fantasy, and lofty values—even childhood fantasy books that will restore lost childlike qualities. Go to see inspiring movies (although those seem to be more difficult to find these days). Avoid mindless violence, sexploitation, and action thrillers. Rather, seek out the classic stories, old and new, that are uplifting to the spirit and portray heroism, love, indomitable spirits, and good comedic fun.

Let yourself laugh, even with slapstick foolishness, and let yourself cry when you are moved by poignant tales. Your spirit thrives on healthy expressions of emotion.

Play with your children, nieces, nephews, or neighborhood kids. Let the child inside you come out to enjoy the simple kinds of play activities that give your children pleasure.

We have a friend who tells how her daughter helped her come alive to the childish joy that had been buried so deeply within her. For several years she found herself dreading her child's appeals to take her to the playground. She would often go begrudgingly and just watch. But with her daughter's insistence, she began to enter in more readily—to swing on the swing set and to push and ride the merry-go-round. The playful activity and sharing in her daughter's joy began to loosen her up emotionally. Soon she began to look forward to the experience. It became refreshing and energizing to her, and she began to discover a new openness and excitement about the small things that previously had gone unnoticed in her world.

We told this story at a meeting where we were speaking, and a woman came up afterward to share a similar spirit-awakening experience that had meant so much to her. She said, "I never received much life-giving attention as a child. I can't remember ever being hugged or played with by my parents. Consequently I had always felt awkward and uncomfortable giving that kind of playful attention to my own children."

She went on to describe how one day, when her grown children had come for a visit, her four-year-old grandson asked if he could play in the motorboat they had on a trailer in their backyard. She rather reluctantly gave him permission, and he quickly climbed aboard, grabbed the steering wheel, and began making the *Brrrrr! Brrrr!* sounds of a pretend outboard motor. He then turned around and saw her watching. He said, "Grandma, you could play too! You could water ski if you really tried."

At first a little embarrassed at the prospect, she looked around to make sure nobody was watching. Then she took the skis out of the boat, positioned them on the ground, and slipped them onto her feet. As she picked up the towrope, her grandson started up his imaginary motor again and shouted, "Here we go!"

She stood there for a moment with her feet planted in those water skis and the rope in her hand, but then something came over her and she really got into the spirit of the thing. It occurred to her that she had seen a lot of people hit big waves while they were skiing and fall into the water. So she pretended to bounce along with the waves, and then she took a big tumble. Lying on the ground, she cried out to her grandson, "Help me. I've fallen in the water!"

With that, her grandson stopped making his motor sounds, jumped down out of the boat, and pretended to swim over to where she was lying in the grass. As he was helping her to her feet, she glanced up at the house. There were her grown children looking out at her from the kitchen window, laughing uproariously.

In telling this story on herself, she said, "You know, it didn't make any difference that they had seen me do what I ordinarily would have thought was such a foolish thing, because all of a sudden I felt rising up in me a wonderful childlike joy that I had never experienced before. I knew that the Lord was bringing to life in me something that really needed to be awakened."

She got it right! The point is, we shouldn't take life so seriously. If we want to stay alive and vibrant in our personal spirits, we must be kind to ourselves and regularly nurture ourselves with fun activities.

Go back to chapter 6 and review some of the activities you can do with children. Put yourself in the place of a child and do these activities for yourself. (Go ahead. Take a bath by candlelight or with goggles on to keep the soap out of your eyes. Why not?)

Get together more often with Christian friends. Seek out companionship to have a good time talking, sharing, singing, laughing, and playing together. Be real. Be alive.

Take an interest in each other's families. Expand the circle of your love. Pay attention to little things. Take time to celebrate birthdays, anniversaries, special days, and accomplishments. Talk to each other regularly on the phone if you do not have opportunity to meet in person.

Do kind things for each other. Surprise your friends with a pie or cake, or share a recipe. Recommend and share a good book. Ask for advice or a referral to a doctor. Be friendly and be a friend.

Husbands and wives, pour all of your affection out to one another, warmly and openly. It will affirm and revitalize each of you. Give joyously and adventurously to each other in your sex life; it will increase your intimacy and help you come alive.

5. Take care of yourself.

Doctors frequently recommend that patients suffering from stress and nervous tension get regular exercise and become involved in an active recreational activity. That's good advice for the slumbering spirit as well. Get active in a sport or a hobby.

Join a softball team, volleyball team, bowling league, or crafts group. Share in the fellowship. Stretch yourself to be more vulnerable. Risk doing something frivolous and fun. Challenge yourself. Succeed in a project and feel proud. Or fail gloriously and feel humbled and childlike, but happy that you tried. Exhaust yourself with exercise, and then glory in a wonderful steamy shower and a good night's sleep between freshly laundered sheets.

Diet is also very important. Avoid fatty, heavily sugared, and junk foods. Eat plenty of fresh fruits and vegetables. Eat in moderation. Stay away from stimulants and depressants. That means avoiding caffeine, nicotine, and alcohol. Particularly beware of marijuana or other mind-altering drugs. These put your spirit into a deeper slumber than ever before.

6. Read good Christian literature.

Bookstores and libraries have a wealth of good books from which to choose, ranging from religious classics to contemporary poetry and inspirational works. Discover the richness of biographies of great Christian leaders in history. Explore Christian family values and challenge yourself to define a personal ethical stance. This will help you focus on self-discovery, personal devotions, and inspiration.

Participate in guided Bible study, focusing on the ways God could be speaking to you through the Scriptures. Avoid fastening onto the "shoulds" and the "oughts" that tighten you into striving. See and celebrate the very real passions and emotions of biblical characters.

Write down meaningful quotes you come across. Stick them on your refrigerator or bulletin board. Let them become a part of your life. Share good ideas and inspirational thoughts with friends.

Express yourself. Keep a journal to jot down your thoughts and prayers daily. Write your own brief psalms of praise for the little things in life that give you pleasure and for which you can thank God. Celebrate good ideas that inspire you.

7. Get involved in nature, music, and art.

Large doses of nature are a tonic to the spirit. Get outside and take walks in the park or the woods. Go camping or fishing.

Walk along the seashore and hunt for shells or driftwood. Go out at night and study the stars. Pay attention to the beauty of sunrises and sunsets. Experience how big and how wonderful God's creation is.

Listen to good music that will relax you, stimulate your imagination, or inspire you spiritually. Also, surround yourself with good art. Spend time in museums, art galleries, or viewing art books that will awaken your creative interests.

7. Touch and be touched.

Practice making eye-to-eye contact whenever you talk to other people. Don't be afraid to take another person's hand, touch them in friendship on the arm or shoulder, or hug them in greeting or in saying good-bye. Encourage group togetherness by physically touching each other in times of prayer. Bless each other with the laying on of hands.

Hug your children, even though it may feel awkward to you or perhaps you feel that they are too old for that kind of expression. (They aren't!) Put your arm around them when you walk or talk with them. Relax and express yourself to them physically.

Be honest with yourself about your thoughts and feelings. Discern in your own mind the difference between sexual attraction and wholesome expressions of love and friendship. Ask Jesus to take the lust from your struggling mind and put it to death on the cross so that you might enter into relationships with pure motives and without the baggage of hidden sexual agendas.

Face up to your sexual vulnerability, and let God help you overcome temptation through prayer. Pray for the transformation of your mind into wholesome feelings about physical contact.

8. Get involved in helping others.

Don't just focus on your own needs. Learn to give as well as take. If you want others to be there for you, then be willing to be there for them. Stay aware. Ministry to others in need will do much to help you rethink the priorities in your own life and to put your needs into proper perspective. The only danger here is if you escape into a total focus on other people's needs and do not also tend to your own spirit.

9. Ask a friend to pray with you for your healing.

⤸ Ask your heart to forgive those who did not give you nurture, and pray for healing of

those hidden yet destructive wounds to the
spirit.

⊰ Pray for your heart of stone to be softened
and for a renewed sense of love and concern
for others.

⊰ Pray to be released from your inner vows
that shield you from being vulnerable to
others (such as, "I won't need the hugs I
never received," "I won't need the play I
never experienced," "I won't share my heart,
since no one ever showed an interest in me,"
and so on). Trust that the pain of being more
open will bring much greater rewards of
friendship and renewed trust.

⊰ Pray for the Holy Spirit to guide you on a
journey of new discovery to awaken to the
simple joys of life and to the wonder of deep-
ened personal relationships.

⊰ Pray for others and ask them to pray for you.
Pray with confidence that God has the power
to transform you and that through the cross
of Jesus Christ you will overcome all difficul-
ties. Pray that your spirit will come alive in
new awareness and new vitality.

Talk to God at every opportunity through flash prayers throughout the day. Develop an attitude of prayer. Listen to what God may be saying to you in return. Pay attention to your dreams that are unusually vivid or come repeatedly. Learn what they mean to you.

Start each day with an "out-loud" prayer in which you enthusiastically choose life, openness, relationships, love, vibrancy, and fun. If indeed we are what we think, then make your thought patterns for the day a prayer of positive affirmations to God. Tell yourself and God that you will think and behave in ways that exemplify a fully awakened personal spirit.

Pay whatever price of self-discipline, trust, vulnerability, and personal pain that is necessary in order to come alive. Jesus said He came to give us life, and that more abundantly. Seek it!

> *Lord,*
>
> *Give me the courage to break out of familiar patterns and to try new resources for refreshment and growth. Help me to let go of rigid, overburdening seriousness.*
>
> *Teach me to play so that the child in me has a chance to live.*
>
> *Enable me to choose life continually, in my prayer discipline and in my attitudes and actions toward myself and others.*

Give me the strength of spirit to take the initiative to reach out to people—to let them know me and minister to me, as well as to make myself available to know and to minister to them. Help me to live in the joy of Your loving grace. Amen.

CHAPTER 7 AWAKENING EXERCISES

1. Review the suggested personal inventory in this chapter to explore ways in which your spirit may be asleep. Discuss with your group or a friend the areas in which you need the most rejuvenation.

2. Think through and write out a personal plan of spiritual renewal by describing actions you will take for each of the following suggestions. Be sure you take action in each area at least once a week.

   Seek affection in my own family.

   I will:

   _____

   _____

   Seek out Christian friends who can understand, support, and confront me in love.

   I will:

   _____

   _____

Seek ways to lighten my heart through fun.

I will:

_____

_____

Take care of myself through sleep, exercise, and diet.

I will:

_____

_____

Read good Christian devotional literature.

I will:

_____

_____

Get involved in nature, music, and art.

I will:

_____

_____

Touch and be touched in Christian fellowship.

I will:

_____

_____

Get involved in helping others.

I will:

_____

_____

Ask others to pray with me for my own inner healing.

I will:

_____

_____

Consider how each of the actions you have listed can be worked into your weekly and daily schedule. Actually put them on your calendar as a reminder to seek these ways to awaken your spirit.

8

Nurture Through Family, Friends, and Small Groups

THERE ARE TWO KINDS OF FAMILIES THAT WE consider to be very important in waking the slumbering spirit: our natural family into which we were born and the family of God through which we share a kinship through faith in Jesus Christ. We have said much about the importance of the natural family assuming God-intended responsibility for spiritual nurture that produces fully human men and women. That nurturing is essentially accomplished, or not accomplished, in the early years of a child's life.

If a natural family imparts love, affection, touching, and spiritual nurture, the natural and effervescent personal spirit within children can be kept alive as they grow into adulthood. If, however, the spirit fails to be nurtured or later falls into a slumbering state through sin, neglect of worship, or the seduction of a spiritually impoverished lifestyle, awakening must come through the help of individuals and small groups of friends who, by their own lively presence, can renurture one back to life.

I (Lee) experienced this in a very dramatic way during a time in my life when my spirit was at a very low ebb. The stress of life circumstances had me depressed, emotionally exhausted, and consumed with negative thinking. I was like the cartoon character who walks around with a rain cloud hovering just above his head. Then, when I least expected it, I was confronted by the glowing personality of a person I could not ignore (and who eventually became my wife). Despite my seeming desire to remain in isolation, alone, dark, and cold, she allowed the light and joy of the Lord to shine through her. Her happiness was a much-needed shock to my personal spirit, and years later my spirit was well into recovery.

Friends cannot forcefully shake someone awake any more than a sinner can be harassed into contrition. Scolding, criticism, or advice will likely produce the opposite of desired results. What is needed is the lively example of those who have a zest for life and who will surround a person with love, cheerful optimism, faithful friendship, and encouragement.

If natural family members are also slumbering in their spirits and are unaware, then the extended family of God must assume the role as nurturing agents to bring about awakening. This is not a quick and easy process and should not be expected to come as an instant miracle of transformation.

Awakening cannot be accomplished by others for us; it requires our own determination, bolstered by the continuous love and encouragement of others. Friends and family need to recognize that waking the slumbering spirit most often will be a long journey with two steps forward and one step back. It will be a journey with many confusing branches in the road and much fog to obscure the vision. But it is a journey of infinite worth for both the pilgrim and the guides.

The awareness and the choice to seek an awakening must come from within the individual person. It is best encouraged by identifying with and living amidst a gentle, loving, and fun-filled community of friends.

For an adult coming into the realization that his spirit is slumbering, the best source of help is through the loving nurture of a small group. Every Christian congregation should have cell groups dedicated to Bible study, prayer, inner healing, and service projects that direct their energies outward.

Small groups are where "church" really happens because that is where the work of Christ is done in the world. Small groups are where God becomes incarnate through love. Small groups allow the power of the Holy Spirit to work in true corporateness where the grace of God comes alive and is applied to the lives of people to heal wounds caused by sin and neglect.

There is no greater gift a family member or a friend can bestow than to involve a loved one in a small group that can love him back to life. Groups will be imperfect, and not every group will be the right fit, but it is worth the search to find the right combination of Christian people to administer the rejuvenation of God's grace.

GUIDELINES TO HELP SMALL CHRISTIAN GROUPS REACH THEIR HEALING POTENTIAL

1. Establish a regular meeting time and expectation of attendance.

Relationship building requires presence, both physically and emotionally. If a group is to be productive, it must meet regularly enough for members to gain weekly sustenance from each other and to have a sense from day to day about what is going on in the lives of those involved.

It is good for a group to make a real commitment about certain ground rules. The first of these should be a commitment to be present whenever possible and to come, not as an observer, but with willingness to share from one's heart.

Meet at the same place for the first six weeks or so to enhance the group's bonding. Share the expense of hiring a teenager to look after the children while you meet. Or you could rotate child care among group members by dropping off children at one location and taking turns.

Atmosphere at group meetings can be very important. Bright lights and big rooms are not conducive to sharing. Find an agreeable meeting place that is quiet, free from distractions, and has a feeling of intimacy. A home is ideal if it can be free from the telephone ringing and the children interrupting.

If you must meet in a church classroom, go to one corner, put down a throw rug, plug in a floor lamp, and turn off the overhead lights. Also be sure to sit close to each other to create a feeling of togetherness and so everyone can be seen and heard.

2. Select a competent leader/facilitator for best results.

Total spontaneity and shared leadership in small groups is not without successful precedent. However, if a recognized leader is available to facilitate the process, the group is much more likely to stay focused, on track, productive, and happy.

The ideal facilitator, of course, would be a trained Christian counselor or prayer minister who is experienced in group dynamics, familiar with the principles of inner healing, and has the confidence of all group members. But few groups will have the good fortune of such enlightened leadership. If a group gets stuck on single issues, seems always out of control, or is inconsistent and inattentive to evident needs, it is probably a sign of lack of leadership.

A minimum requirement for successful groups is to choose from among the members one who is equipped to serve as an organizer or shepherd, make arrangements, facilitate the program, and direct the sharing time to keep the group as focused and constructive as possible. A good leader is one who can comfortably share from his or her own life and who is interested in and respectful of the participation of everyone in the group.

Group leadership may be shared—with each member exercising his best gifts to provide administration, hospitality, music, teaching, wise counsel, or special kinds of ministry. Whatever is done, the group should focus on helping each member be his or her best self and gain the maximum benefit from the time spent together.

Lay leadership can be very effective in most group settings. However, there are types of problems among group members that should not be dealt with unless under the leadership of a trained prayer minister or professional counselor.

Group members should recognize that alcoholism, drug addiction, sexual abuse, and physical abuse are hard issues that require special care and training. Layperson-led small groups should not undertake the task of providing major kinds of ongoing therapy related to problems that should be dealt with in professional Christian counseling. Otherwise, the group will become too focused on extreme situations it cannot adequately handle and that rob others with lesser needs of the opportunity for healing and growth.

3. Include a time of worship and singing.

Group time should always include a time of inspiration and fun, a time to be renewed in fellowship, and a time to recharge one's spiritual batteries. Devotional worship and sharing through song is an excellent way to maintain that focus. Worship and song also prepare everyone's spirit to hear messages from God and to be tuned in to the spirits of others in the group.

Groups can also profit by planning times that are designed for pure recreation. Picnics, outings, concerts, and other events held for the fun of getting together provide the relaxed fellowship that will help group members bond in different ways. These events are a good time to establish relationships with the families of other members so you can all know and understand each other on a deeper level.

4. Conduct some kind of objective study on an appropriate topic that will both interest and inform group members.

The infusion of fresh, new, and well-honed ideas through a time of study will keep the group from focusing exclusively on the heavy issues of its own members' needs. However, be careful so as not to get overly caught up in the study and flee into the "safe objectivity" of it to avoid dealing with needed personal issues. Times of Bible study or book study should contribute to the sharing and healing process, but they cannot be a substitute for it.

If a study is undertaken, the leader should always be careful to call for personal application of the ideas presented. He or she should always challenge the group to consider how ideas can be translated to action:

- How can this idea make a difference in my life?

- How can I apply this to solve a problem, heal a hurt, enable repentance, or awaken my slumbering spirit?

5. Be honest and real in group relationships.

Open and honest discussion of life concerns is essential if a small group is to succeed. Unless group members are accustomed to sharing from the heart, it may be difficult for them to do anything but make easy conversation about issues of no consequence. Or some individuals may be willing to deal with issues other people share, but they are reluctant at first to speak up and reveal their own needs and concerns.

For group members to warm up to one another, it is best to start sharing with simple, open requests to which everyone can respond; for example, "Tell me about one of your fondest childhood memories." Or perhaps: "Describe the person and the place that represented the center of emotional warmth to you when you were growing up."

From there you can move on to deeper and perhaps more painful issues that could be dealt with in a healing way by the group.

If nobody else in the group is sharing from their heart, take the lead and say, "Let me tell you my story and my problems. I want you to pray for me."

Usually when one person starts, it breaks open like a flood, and others will share. Once people learn that the group is a safe place to share, they will participate with growing enthusiasm. More and more, they will want to open up and share with real honesty what is going on inside them.

6. Be open to new people coming into the group.

Although effective groups are built around people who have learned (oftentimes through struggle) to relate well to each other and are willing to be there for mutual support, avoid shutting new members out. The concept of a group that grows like a cell, continually giving birth to other groups, is a healthy model to emulate. A group can become too closed, too much of a clique, and too inbred to continue vibrant growth among its members. Bringing new people into the relationships is almost always very healthy.

We've been in several groups where, once that basic trust of openness and sharing was established, new people could come into the group without deterring the old members from sharing, and once the new people saw what was happening, they would immediately be open as well. It is amazing how quickly that happens.

Our experience is that when a group grows to twelve or more people, the usual problems of group dynamics begin to happen—a few do all the talking. Groups should have an apprentice facilitator who can learn and practice various group-dynamic skills. Then, leadership is available when it is time for a parent group to birth a second group. Smaller groups are more manageable, more productive, and are more able to welcome new members.

Particularly within the church family, the occasional rotation of members between various share groups will create a healthy unity within the diversity and promote sharing throughout the congregation.

Lyman Coleman, author, lecturer, and creator of the well-known Serendipity small-group movement, teaches that groups need to discover a purpose beyond themselves within a year of their organization. If groups do not get into ministry of some sort or parent another group and welcome new members, they tend to become dysfunctional.

Coleman frequently uses the technique of placing an empty chair at group meetings. This is a purposeful reminder to members that they need to reach out to others and bring them in to benefit from the healing and growth that can come through small-group relationships. Small groups can accomplish healing, ministry, and evangelism at its very best.

7. Stay aware of possible discomfort in group dynamics.

Recognize that some group members will have very strong needs and will require and even demand a lot of attention. This can cause a discomfort level for others. When people have been raised in very dysfunctional families, they will seek answers to their needs in whatever kind of small group they find.

If the group is enlightened about what the slumbering spirit is, they can more easily recognize what is going on when a person objectifies or projects a lot of suppressed anger and frustration, now surfacing from childhood, onto certain people within the group. When this happens, group members don't have to take it as a personal offense and react. They can recognize that the person needs some unconditional love, and they can give it.

Certain "shame" issues also may be present among group members. This is often the case with victims of incest or sexual or physical abuse; persons formerly involved in homosexuality; or adult children of alcoholics. To deal with these particularly sensitive areas, the group may have to agree within itself on a boundary system to establish rules of how far to probe and a referral system to handle crises.

Members should come into the group recognizing that it will not be all pleasant fellowship and lighthearted good times. There may be honest hurts and angers expressed and confrontations needed. The group may not be fully competent to handle every situation and may need to recommend one-on-one professional Christian counseling or prayer ministry. Love is the key. The group must hang together in loving commitment and be willing to work through the rough times to accomplish healing.

8. Don't be afraid to establish needed boundaries.

Occasionally a person who has wanted parenting and has never received it may tend to latch onto a mother or father figure within the church or the small group and consequently ask too much of them. This kind of overwhelming need may become very demanding. The spiritual mother and father figures may feel as if they are being eaten alive and should set boundaries for their own emotional protection.

If some parameters are to be drawn, simply say, "I care about you and want to spend time with you, but your need for attention is inordinate. I can't allow you to occupy all my time, just as I wouldn't for one of my natural children." The group member hungry for spiritual parenting must learn through verbal teaching how to be appropriate in the search for meaningful nurture.

9. Respect the confidentiality of what is shared in the group.

In order to share with others from their hearts, group members want to be able to trust that their confessions and expressions of need will be held in confidence by others and not be discussed outside the group.

The only exception to this might be in the discovery of sexual or physical abuse. In such cases there is a legal and moral responsibility to take whatever action is needed to prevent further endangerment of the victim, particularly if children are involved. Groups should act with Christian grace to provide comfort, counsel, and protection for the abused and find professional help for the abuser.

10. Recognize that true healing is not accomplished by our doing, but by God's Holy Spirit, working through His church, facilitated through prayer.

Change in a person's life cannot happen without an acknowledgment of need and a desire to be different. However, recognition of a wounded and slumbering spirit does not assure that healing will happen. Many people stay in private therapy for years and become very enlightened about their psychological state. But healing is not accomplished without the grace of forgiveness and repentance and the transformation of the inner person through the presence of the Holy Spirit.

Christians forming small groups for the purpose of healing wounds, waking slumbering spirits, and sustaining each other in love must recognize that they have the power of the church. It is not their power. It is the power of God incarnate in them through the Holy Spirit who can work miracles of love in the lives of people.

Prayer is essential. Prayer is the way in which God and man are joined in open communication and through which the healing power of God pours out through loving relationships among Christian friends.

Small groups literally can love a slumbering spirit back to life—not by their own power, for it is God who does it through them. Prayer and renurturing love are the dynamic forces through which healing and spiritual awakening are accomplished.

11. Recognize and celebrate growth among group members.

As real personal growth begins to happen, group members need to recognize how individuals are coming alive and acknowledge their growth openly through affirmations, compliments, and encouragement. The group can celebrate the unfolding of rejuvenated personal spirits and share as a group in that joy.

> The creation waits in eager anticipation for the sons of God to be revealed.
>
> —Romans 8:19

> Let us hold unswervingly to the hope we profess, for he who promised is faithful. And let us consider how we may spur one another on toward love and good deeds.
>
> —Hebrews 10:23–24

12. Exhibit the fruit of the Spirit, and do not fear moving on to new relationships.

In all that you do, keep in mind those basic life-principles that Paul described as fruit of God's Spirit working in you. As you relate to each other for inner healing and to awaken the slumbering spirit, you can do no better than to care for each other in:

- Love
- Joy
- Peace
- Patience
- Kindness
- Goodness
- Faithfulness
- Gentleness
- Self-control

When a group is truly bonded in love and support, a time will come when members move from sharing their own stories to a higher and more intimate plane—creating the group's own unique story by becoming a community. True community evokes wonderful feelings of joy and security that we may be tempted to grasp too tightly for fear they will slip away.

Yet the amazing dynamic of real community among persons with awakened personal spirits is that the accompanying catharsis and bonding allow them to release each other to move on to new places, new experiences, and maturity in Christ. (See Ephesians 4:11–16.)

Do not be fearful of leaving behind a small group of dear supportive friends who have helped you to become more fully human. The bonding of past relationships is never lost. As Lyman Coleman says, bonded relationships continue to function "on call" for a lifetime. Everyone then has the freedom to build an ever-widening circle of friends with whom to share love and nurture for a richer and more fulfilling life.

> *Heavenly Father,*
>
> *Thank You for the good and positive things our earthly parents have given us. Thank You also that we never have to be stuck with the negative and hurtful experiences of our lives. We don't have to make do with a starvation diet or a twisted and distorted image of who we are. Jesus can make all things new.*
>
> *Increase the glory of my new birth in You. I want to be fully free and alive in the family of God where Jesus can have opportunity to love and heal and nurture me through relationships with mothers and fathers, sisters and brothers, grandparents, aunts, uncles, and cousins in the Lord.*
>
> *I want to be fully a part of Your family, Lord, rooted in love and growing in every way to become all that You have created me to be.*

I trust You to love others to fullness of life through me. Help me never to focus on the imperfections of those around me, but rather to always focus on You—beginning a good work in us today and surely perfecting it in us until the day of Christ Jesus. Amen.

CHAPTER 8 AWAKENING EXERCISES

1. Do you feel a need to be a member of a small group of Christians who can provide nurture for you? If so, identify the three most basic needs you would like a group to fulfill.

_____

_____

_____

2. Identify three contributions you believe you could bring to a group to help make it an effective healing environment for you and for others.

_____

_____

_____

3. Identify and describe a time in your life when you felt the most involved, loved, happy, and spiritually fulfilled.

_____

_____

_____

4. List the three most important elements that contributed to those good feelings.

_____

_____

_____

5. Seriously consider these questions: "What would it take to create the proper kind of environment in which to grow spiritually in my life today? What kind of persons should I seek? Where should I seek them? What will I have to do to help stimulate the kind of nurturing I need?" Jot down your ideas:

_____

_____

_____

_____

_____

_____

6. Discuss these issues with a friend or with the group you are already in. Then write out a personal plan of action to which you are willing to commit yourself.

Actions I will take to seek nurturing friendships:

_____

_____

Places I will go to find the right kind of friends:

_____

_____

Actions I will take to stimulate my own nurtured growth and spirit awakening:

_____

_____

7. Review your plan of action once a month. Check your-self to determine whether you are remaining "on course." Are you keeping your commitments to yourself? If not, why not?

_____

_____

_____

_____

CONCLUSION

THE REST OF THE STORY

W E ALL CAN USE A REMINDER OCCASIONALLY that some things are not what they at first appear to be—and when we get caught up in foolishness (or just plain being wrong), the best medicine is confession.

We began this book with a story about a wild kitten born in the garage to a wild mother named Fraidie. That kitten, through loving nurture, became the snugly and warm family pet named Lady. The story we told is perfectly true, as is the analogy that each of us needs a similar kind of loving nurture to come into our full humanity with awakened personal spirits. But we cannot let that story end without confessing a later development that humbled us, left us laughing at ourselves, and taught another object lesson as well.

Cat lovers will usually admit there is something special about a sweet little female kitten that makes you feel differently than you do about a tomcat. That's the way we were feeling about Lady. She was so affectionate and frisky. It was so cute how she had learned to jump up on our bed in the mornings to wake us by pushing her head beneath our hands, asking to be petted to start her day and ours.

When she was about six months old, she went through a period of about three days in which she began acting rather strange and agitated. We thought at first that she was just bridging her adolescence and was experiencing her first period of being in heat. But this particular morning, as we were ruffling her soft fur there on the bed, we had quite a surprise. We discovered that this sweet little female kitten was not a lady at all. Virtually overnight, in what appeared to be some latent gland development, Lady produced the unmistakable evidence that she was really a teenage tom!

Our first response was, "This is unbelievable!" Then, "How embarrassing!" Finally, "How will we muster the nerve to tell our friends that we can't tell the difference between a male and a female cat?"

After half a day of shaking our heads in shock and self-doubt, we regained some composure by remembering that this kitten had been to the vet to get an exam and the usual series of shots. If the vet hadn't questioned why we would name a male kitten Lady, then maybe he was confused too. Why should we feel so bad?

That afternoon, Lady was renamed "Grady." During the next few days a rather remarkable thing began to happen. We started thinking of Grady in new ways. Yes, he was still the sweet, cuddly, frisky, and affectionate kitten we had known as Lady. But he somehow seemed less feminine now that we knew he was not a female. We began to play with him differently. Instead of thinking of him as a cute and coy little female cat, we began to call him a "little rascal"—a decidedly masculine perception.

"Isn't that strange?" we commented. And then with a little deeper thought we wondered aloud: "Maybe that's more of a comment on us than it is on Grady, who, after all, was just being his same sweet self!"

If the Fraidie-Lady analogy holds true to illustrate the power of loving nurture, then perhaps the Lady-Grady episode can teach us something as well. Maybe the end result of nurture is determined in large measure by how one is perceived by others and how one ultimately comes to perceive one's self.

Did Grady become a sweet and loving cat because we treated him as a kitten as we perceived him (or her) to be? If we had initially perceived him to be a tom and had treated him more rough-and-tumble, or perhaps more distantly macho, would he have turned out differently? Probably!

We can learn lessons here on several levels. First, we should carefully evaluate how we perceive and treat our children; for example, do we automatically go into autopilot to raise our girls as sweeties and our boys as toughies? Or can we appreciate strength in women and tenderness in men and allow these qualities to develop naturally in our children no matter what their gender?

It is likely that our children will rise to the highest level of our expectations if we love them properly, give them room to learn and grow, and consistently administer God's grace.

Secondly, do we recognize in ourselves how our reactions to the nurturing environment in which we have lived have done much to produce our own self-concept? Do we recognize the extent to which the perceptions we have of ourselves were shaped by our reactions to the treatment and attitudes of others? Have we gone to sleep spiritually because we have closed our hearts in sinful reaction to inadequate nurture, neglect, and our own lack of understanding how to stay fully alive?

Most importantly, do we know how to get beyond those limitations to begin to grow instead into who God wants us to be as our best selves? Do we understand how important it is to find Christian friends who will love, nurture, and encourage? Do we understand how God desires for us to be fully awake, sensitive to His voice, and responsive to His Spirit in our lives?

If there is but one lingering message that should be understood by reading this book, it is that you do not have to live your life as a victim.

No matter what my journey has been, no matter what nurturing or lack of nurturing I have experienced, no matter what pain and scars I bear—from this moment on, life is a choosing.

Rise and shine, you sleeping spirits! Like Grady, the wild kitten who now so dearly loves the stroking hand, do not fear asking for affection that will nourish and refresh. Venture out into new territories, secure in the protection of a God who loves you and will surely be your guide.

NOTES

CHAPTER 2
WHAT CAUSES THE SPIRIT TO SLUMBER

1. Marian Wright Edelman, *The Measure of Our Success* (Boston, MA: Beacon Press, 1992), 19.

CHAPTER 6
NURTURING YOUR CHILD'S SPIRITUAL VITALITY

1. Jean Grasso Fitzpatrick, *Something More, Nurturing Your Child's Spiritual Growth* (New York: Viking, 1991).

2. Adele Faber and Elaine Mazlish, *How to Talk So Kids Will Listen and Listen So Kids Will Talk* (New York: Avon, 1990).

3. Ibid.

GLOSSARY OF COMMON TERMS

NOAH WEBSTER WORKED DILIGENTLY FOR OVER thirty years to assemble the dictionary that we generally accept as the standard for academic use today. Putting together a universally acceptable dictionary of theological terms would perhaps be even more difficult. Our intention is to help readers understand in a very basic way some of the key theological terms used in this book. Please accept it for what it is and read with Christian grace.

body—the flesh and blood of one's earthly form, spiritually linked as the dwelling place (temple) of one's mind, soul, and personal spirit

body of Christ—the Church universal, including all persons who have confessed that Jesus Christ is the Son of God and have committed themselves to follow Him as their Lord and Savior

born again—a term describing one who has repented of sin, received the forgiving grace of Jesus Christ, and commits to walk in newness of life through the power of His death, burial, and resurrection

charismatic—a born-again Christian who recognizes and personally utilizes the unique gifts of God's Holy Spirit with which he or she is equipped to do the work of Christ in the world for the edification of Christ's Church

Church—all those who confess Jesus as Christ, the Messiah, Son of the one true God, and who join together in fellowship to do God's work

conscience—a *true conscience* is activated through an awakened personal spirit to allow one to empathize with the possible hurt to another person or one's self. It provides a warning ahead of time to avoid actions that will cause hurt of injustice. A *remorse conscience* works after an event as a reminder of wrongs committed. It is activated primarily on the basis of rules or laws broken, or on regret for having been caught—not out of empathy for one who might have been hurt by one's action.

evangelical—a person who knows, has experienced, and teaches what it is to be born again in Jesus Christ

family of God—all persons, whether blood relatives or not, who consciously contribute to the spiritual nurture of others out of the love and unity they feel as followers of Jesus Christ

fruit of the Spirit—the attitudes and actions that result from the presence of the Holy Spirit in the Christian's life (love, joy, peace, patience, kindness, goodness, faithfulness, gentleness, and self-control, as seen in Galatians 5:22-23)

Holy Spirit—the spiritual presence of God who is three in one (Father, Son, and Holy Spirit) who dwells among us to convict us of sin, call us into repentance and salvation, comfort us in need, and empower us to do His work in the world

human animal—by purely scientific definition, humans are members of the animal kingdom that fit the classification of mammals since they are warm blooded, produce milk to feed offspring born alive, and have body hair. The "human animal," however, is uniquely distinguished from other animals by virtue of the fact that humans are created in God's image and animals are not. Thus, humans are much higher than animals.

human—to have an awakened personal spirit by which we identify and empathize with others, becoming one with them and cherishing what is in the other person even more than our own life. In short, being fully human is to be like Jesus.

humanism—the glorification of the human position, placing man as the crown of the universe, becoming ever more elevated in intellect and relationships based on his rational thought and good works. Humanism stands as a fleshly imitation of what God, the Creator and Sustainer of all life, is doing to transform men and women into the character of Jesus Christ through His saving grace.

Incarnation, the—the act of God in which He actually became human flesh through Jesus Christ that all persons might be brought into restored relationship with Him. Persons share in the Incarnation as they profess Jesus Christ as Savior and allow God's Holy Spirit to take control of their lives to do the work of Christ in the world.

inner healing—the healing of spiritual and emotional wounds resulting in renewed inner peace and the restoration of right relationships with others and with God. Inner healing is accomplished by acknowledging one's sins and woundings, and repenting of judgments against those who have wounded us. We call to death strongholds in the flesh that our judgments have formed in us, forgive others, accept forgiveness, and call the new man to life in Christ. The transforming power of Christ makes all things new by taking the sin and woundings of mankind upon Himself.

inspiration—creative concepts, ideas, insights, understandings, or expressions of feeling that are communicated by God's Spirit through an individual's awakened personal spirit

keys of knowledge—special insights given by God to help persons understand their spiritual condition and to enable them to seek inner healing and spiritual restoration through His grace

mind—our intellect, the reasoning and logical decision-making capacity to choose a course of action

nurture—the cumulative effect of how one loves, cares for, teaches, and sets an example in the shaping of another person's personal spirit, thoughts, feelings, and character

personal spirit—the God-given inner being, the life force within an individual that determines how one relates to others and to God, and how vibrancy of life and quality of soul are developed and maintained

prayer—personal communication with God for the purpose of praise, thanksgiving, seeking help, or interceding for the benefit of others with whom one identifies

prophet—one who has a specific gift from God's Holy Spirit to understand and communicate direct words from God with power, conviction, and clarity

religion—the form or ritual of worship and devotion to God that can be involved in true spirit-to-Spirit relationship with God, but often is focused more on rules, regulations, rituals, and customs than on relationship with God

slumbering spirit—one who through reactions to a lack of proper nurture as a child has closed his heart and has been stunted in his or her ability to relate adequately to others and to God; or who, as an adult, has withdrawn from intimate relationships, withdrawn from art and nature, neglected worship, and fallen into repeated sin, resulting in spiritual and emotional lethargy

soul—the structure of the mind, character, and personality that is developed as one's personal spirit encounters life, reacts, and builds coping mechanisms

speaking in tongues—one of many gifts of God's Holy Spirit, enabling the recipient to praise God or to receive a message from God in a language unknown to the recipient, spirit to Spirit, in a way that circumvents the language patterns or limiting filters of one's conscious mind

spiritual gifts—God's special gifts of enabling power through His Holy Spirit by which Christians are equipped to do the work of Christ in the world for the development of His Church

worship—communication and joyous praise of God inspired by an attitude of reverence, awe, thankfulness, self-giving, and vulnerability, made possible by the inspiration of God's Holy Spirit and our openness to His presence

SUGGESTIONS FOR FURTHER READING

Berg, Elizabeth. *Family Traditions, Celebrations for Holidays and Everyday.* Pleasantville, NY: The Reader's Digest Association, Inc., 1992.

Coleman, Lyman. *Serendipity Small Group Training Manual.* Littleton, CO: Serendipity House, 1991.

Edelman, Marian Wright. *The Measure of Our Success.* Boston, MA: Beacon Press, 1992.

Faber, Adele and Elaine Mazlish. *How to Talk So Kids Will Listen and Listen So Kids Will Talk.* New York: Avon, 1990.

Fitzpatrick, Jean Grasso. *Something More, Nurturing Your Child's Spiritual Growth.* New York: Viking, 1991.

Olsen, Howard J. *Wounded Warriors Chosen Lives: Healing for Vietnam Veterans.* Arlington, Texas: Clear Stream Publishing, 1997.

Sandford, John Loren and Paula, and Lee Bowman. *Choosing Forgiveness.* Lake Mary, Florida: Charisma House, 2007.

Sandford, John Loren and Paula. *God's Power to Change: Healing the Wounded Spirit.* Lake Mary, Florida: Charisma House, 2007.

Sullivan, S. Adams. *The Quality Time Almanac: A Sourcebook of Ideas and Activities for Parents and Kids.* Garden City, New York: Doubleday and Company, Inc., 1986.

Swindoll, Charles R. *The Grace Awakening.* Dallas, TX: Word Publishing, 1990.

For further information, contact:

Elijah House, Inc.
317 N. Pines Road
Spokane Valley, WA 99206
Web site: www.elijahhouse.org